BLACK SALT FOR WHITE EYES

BLACK SALT FOR WHITE EYES

A MEMOIR

NASIHAH JONES

Paperback ISBN 978-1-951937-77-5

Library of Congress Control Number 20209235770

Book design by Colin Rolfe

Epigraph Books
22 East Market Street, Suite 304
Rhinebeck, NY 12572
(845) 876-4861
epigraphps.com

For the black boy I used to be, the one who didn't survive the trap and the one who became the man I am today. For Zayd, Akachi, and every young black male growing up in America today – survive.

NASIHAH JONES

"Mother and Child"
by Nasihah Jones

CONTENTS

FOREWORD

I HAD a hard time putting this book down. Nasihah's description of growing up poor and Black in the drug-infested and gang-dominated streets of Newburgh was so well written that he made you feel as though you were there. The book has a nice flow and is very easy to read. I loved his detailed description of the city streets, the characters involved in his life and also his analysis of how both the education and criminal justice systems are stacked against anyone poor and Black.

He acknowledged the fact that he had several significant people in his life who helped him survive and pull himself up by the bootstraps. His intelligence, good analytical skills and his ability to write have separated him from so many men who have written about their prison life experiences.

His description of his trial was very well done. It showed how, in spite of a good defense lawyer, and a clear case of self defense, he was still convicted of murder. Nasihah's description of how he felt in that situation was nothing short of brilliant. For the first time in my life I understood why a Black kid growing up in Newburgh had to carry a gun. It was quite a revelation.

As a former Superintendent of Prisons Nasihah served time in, I enjoyed reading about his ability to prevent himself from becoming mentally institutionalized. He made use of prison as a time of introspection and self-improvement. I was also impressed with the way he prepared for his parole board appearance.

So many men fail to understand the importance of making the parole commissioners understand their sense of remorse, how they have changed while in prison and what they will do when they are released. Nasihah did his homework and, consequently, was released.

He has the ability to paint pictures with words. His quotes are memorable, as in

"I was a caged bird screaming to deaf ears."

I feel this is a book well worth reading, and one which has an important message for everyone. I would highly recommend it for anyone in the fields of criminal justice, education and urban planning, and any citizen concerned with prison reform.

DAVID MILLER, former Supervising Superintendent for Mid-Hudson State Prisons, who helped the Bard College student Max Kenner start the Bard Prison Initiative 20 years ago when he was superintendent at the Eastern Correctional Facility in Napanoch, NY.

INTRODUCTION

THIS IS a shocking memoir of an intelligent young Black man growing up terrorized every day in Newburgh, New York, and how he got caught like a fly in the spider's web of injustice found by Blacks in many American cities.

Nasihah Jones describes in grim detail the devastating impacts on inner city minorities from the well-intentioned Great Society War on Poverty in the 1960s and 1970s to the 1994 Violent Crime Control Act and its War on Drugs that led to the mass incarceration of two million mostly Black urban young men. He was one of them.

Jones explains in vivid prose his teenage street experience of the fatal influx of crack cocaine, urban gangs and easy access to illegal guns, and how this toxic mixture led to self-destructive Black-on-Black crime in Newburgh and many other American cities. He describes in a psychologically sophisticated way how despair with their low quality inner city schools and joblessness and no hope for a better future lead inner city Black men to attack each other.

This memoir is not just another cry of complaint about urban victimization of minorities in America. Jones is writing his story to shake young Blacks out of their despair, to take responsibility for their own mature behavior, and to educate themselves in American and Black History to escape their ghetto mentality.

Jones is also writing his story to take blindfolds from white readers whose greater opportunities prevent them from seeing the daily misery of Black people living jobless in slumlord housing just a few miles from their white ghettos. And he clearly shows how white prejudice leads to the assumption of Black guilt in our courts too often, in spite of clear evidence from him and witnesses of his legitimate self-defense after being attacked by a man who had threatened three times to kill him.

Jones tells white readers what they don't know about the vicious circle of urban Black poverty and violence so white voters and politicians can better understand inner city realities, and intelligently participate with Black leaders and community people to plan, fund and effectively implement together new concepts of urban renewal that will actually build safe, livable inner cities with public services like good schools and safe streets and housing code enforcement the white majority in America expects from good government.

Finally, why did I help Nasihah Jones by editing his life story and helping him find a publisher? The first reason was to help him tell the truth about unsolved problems of inner cities that both white and Black people do not know or understand. I was shocked by the brutality of daily life in the Black community of Newburgh, just 20 miles from my well-governed white college town of New Paltz, NY, and how little white people know about the life experience of Blacks living near them.

I admired the determination of Nasihah to lead a better life, to overcome his 11 years of prison by constantly reading, writing and drawing and getting a college education during and after prison and then a good job teaching inner city Black students. I respected his graceful and forceful writing, his fine art skills, his quick intelligence, and his courage to speak his truth to white power.

I also have a professional sense of shame for being a young white reporter for the Middletown, NY, Times Herald-Record covering the white establishment in Newburgh in the early 1960s, when I had no idea about the miserable life Black people were suffering in the inner city of Newburgh. Nasihah's life story was indeed for me "Black Salt for White Eyes."

JIM OTTAWAY, JR., Retired Director and Senior V.P. of Dow Jones & Company; Chairman of Ottaway Newspapers subsidiary of Dow Jones

PREFACE

I WAS told by my grade school teacher that I would not live to the age of 21. I was a nonbeliever of most of the things my teachers told me. But their talk about death and how Black boys live short lives I found myself believing. The old timers in my neighborhood called my city "The Graveyard" because on every block someone had been murdered, making my city the per capita murder capital of New York State. There were so many stories of violence in my life that it was like mental conditioning; I considered death to be part of being young and Black in Newburgh. We accepted the possibility of dying young, even the probability that one of us would pull the trigger to take another Black male out of this world.

America had a way of making us feel Black life was cheap and disposable; and we repeated and perpetuated that lie regularly.
Living inside the four walls of the ghetto, the dearth and the sense of despair is forever present. The world around a young Black urban male drives him towards hopelessness and rage. It blinds him to his own destructive course. He is blind to the white imagination of a future world that does not contain his kind. In the eyes of whites, the future would be much safer that way.

Urban Black males with guns committing genocide of their own people are cutting themselves off from a better future. But we refuse to call it what it is. We refuse to give it a name. The ghetto is too powerless and too apolitical to name it. So we depend on white eyes that watch us from the periphery of the ghetto and accept their name for it—"Black on Black crime."

But there can no longer be a denial of the black salt of this earth. "Ye are the salt of the earth; but if the salt have lost its savour, wherewith shall it be salted? It is thenceforth good for nothing, but to be cast out, and to be trodden under foot of men." (Matthew 5:13).

NASIHAH JONES

CHAPTER 1

BLACK FLIES IN AMERICA

MY STORY begins unfortunately inside what some have called The Belly of the Beast. Yes, I am referring to prison. I was not born inside a prison literally – unless we all agree that America means prison, poetically suggested by brother Malcolm X. I was born American but I wasn't born free. By the age of 15 I was incarcerated inside America's prison system. I was a lost teen. I was a lost child. I was food for America because in the 1990s, America ate its own children. Especially the ones who were brown and Black and particularly those children from urban slums who themselves had digested narratives of American violence. We ate from this tree of American violence, often times because it was the only thing available to feed ourselves. Popular culture served it. Public school systems served it. We consumed, internalized, and regurgitated this violence in our own neighborhoods. Then America turned around and ate us. She devoured her bastard children and locked them away.

I surmise that America is ashamed of us. She is ashamed to show the rest of the world what she has given birth to, what she has raised. And we the Black children of America, those who have survived, are supposed to be silent and inarticulate. We aren't supposed to tell any story that implicates America as an educator of violence. Some of us children could never connect enough dots in our own lives to begin to make sense of all this. I could tell this story only because I lived it, I witnessed it, I spent every day of a decade in prison making sense of it all. I was there when urban violence was reportedly so out of control that the Federal Government passed legislation to purge the streets clean of young Black men (the 1994 Violent Crime Control and Law Enforcement Act).

But it was inside the belly of America where I found my voice. So much of who I am today and where I am today was made while in prison. Although there is nothing romantic about the discussion of prison life, and most people will find appalling the fact that I spent 11 years of my young life inside a prison, it is true that my own experience in prison allowed me to see myself in a larger context, that had I not been in prison, I would never have seen.

Prison is a damaging experience that aims to crush the human soul. Prisons have to be thought about in the same way that we imagine concentration camps and chattel slavery. The experience is comparable to both institutions. We have millions of men and women removed from their communities and sent off to strange and dark spaces that stifle their freedom. They are denied the rights of others and reduced to a state-issued prison number that replaces their birth name. Every day they are corralled and expected to move about like pigs on a farm. The prisoners' humanity and the humanity of the prison guards is suspended and nonexistent. Prisoners are treated like animals but oddly, prisoners refer to their guards as pigs and turnkeys. People lose themselves in prison. They lose their identity. Their humanity is crushed and some become monsters. Many are emotionally institutionalized and their minds draw parallels between the streets and prison until all differences are no more and they find comfort being in prison. These brothers and sisters are the bitter expression of what incarceration does to people. After serving their time behind bars, prisoners are released to their communities. Many are released without a resume, proper job skills training or family and community support. And when they do apply for employment, they discover that their felony status is a permanent mark of shame that further strips away their God-given right to be whole persons, full citizens of America.

But I immediately fought against the mechanical nature of the institution and I found myself by confronting a reality that I was never supposed to be able to define. That reality is the mental illness that all Blacks suffer from. It develops from the trauma caused by the oppression of white supremacy and racism. It is the trauma of being Black in America, where before we can learn to love ourselves we first are taught to hate ourselves and to reject any and everything that is Black.

My story is about this trauma. It is about the mental illness resulting from oppression that most of us will never have the power or the language to define. This mental illness is a kind of insanity within some Blacks that goes unnoticed their entire lives. I'm no clinical psychologist but I have come to understand things that are pertinent to my own experience and survival as a Black man in American society and while I was incarcerated. I have come to understand how oppression and racism work and how internalized racism manifests itself in Black psychology. For years I have contemplated this and have finally found the language to articulate these ideas. To be metaphoric, this Black insanity is like a black fly repeatedly trying to steal crumbs from a spider's web. The fly is fully aware that the spider's web is a trap set up specifically to capture it. And despite the millions of black flies that were already trapped by the spider's web, the fly develops a love for the trap, against its own best interest, and continues to fly into the trap, getting itself killed.

In many of our Black communities, we represent this black fly and we ignore the traps that are set up all around us. We fly directly into the web of white supremacy. Each time we kill ourselves in an attempt to steal away anything that will give us sustenance and make us feel whole. Many of us will find ourselves robbing and killing just to redeem a long lost manhood or womanhood that isn't so easily earned by bar mitzvahs and sweet sixteens. Many of us will indeed die young. Some of us will end up inside the prison system and will be further dehumanized until we are totally broken, irreparable and erased.

My story begins in prison but it does not end there. It starts there only because it was in prison where a light bulb went off inside my head. In that moment I realized I needed to change myself before spending the rest of my life behind bars. Because of where I grew up, I didn't have the comfort of peacefully experiencing my teens. And suddenly, I'm standing in front of a judge who was prepared to sentence me to life in prison. That same judge informed me that I was so reprehensible that I could never be part of a graduating class or attend my high school prom or ever see a college campus in my lifetime. He said that I would never have children of my own and that I would more than likely die in prison. I became that black fly caught in the web of a white miscarriage of justice. I was given a life sentence and condemned to prison for trying to defend myself, for trying to survive within the insanity of the Black ghetto. I became trapped trying to live. This is my story. This is my memoir of how I stopped flying into the web of my own destruction.

CHAPTER 2

PRISON PAROLE CHATTER

I WAS nine years into my sentence when I stood before the parole board for the first time to determine if I was suitable for society after almost a decade in prison. I would not receive my decision until two days after the hearing. You really couldn't understand how I felt unless you were in my shoes. Something as natural as freedom was now in the hands of the State Parole Board. During the two days after the hearing I tried to paint and read to keep myself from thinking about what could possibly happen next. I could be granted my freedom and this nightmare of mine would be over just like that. But I was already deep in the system, with years of prison experience to know that freedom is the hardest thing to regain once you lose it. I had witnessed way too many times the denial of parole to deserving prisoners, so my hopes were far from high. I had spent nine difficult years in the belly of the beast, but freedom had never vanished from my mind. After all those years I could still smell and feel freedom. I fought with myself to stop my body and mind from ever becoming accustomed to life in jail. I had yearned for it every day for the past 3,285 days and counting. I didn't belong in prison. Others probably did. But I did not. I was a victim of a clear miscarriage of justice. Yet I was still convicted and condemned to a nine years to life sentence as a juvenile.

Prison is a gigantic cage where those incarcerated are treated like animals and are expected to act like animals. Behind prison walls, any information connecting us to the outside world is scarce. Newspapers are prohibited and of course cell phones and the Internet. What goes on in prison becomes the only world that prisoners know, and even if they have access to visitors or phone calls to family and friends, the physical barriers are constant reminders that we are not free. The System tries so hard to keep us from experiencing freedom in any meaningful way. Limiting our ability to feel free was the System's way of continuing our punishment after sentencing.

Some prisoners became so used to prison that they long ago forgot what freedom felt like and had no yearning for it. They were the institutionalized prisoners who could no longer see or think beyond prison walls. Their ability to self-reflect and engage in ideas that could possibly transform them was absent. Day-to-day prison life was their only concern.

Prison gossip and rumors were like CNN to many prisoners. Gossip about another prisoner's affairs seemed to make days in prison less unbearable. Either that or prisoners spent hours engaged in meaningless arguments about the lives of celebrities and entertainers. Their fantasies somehow allowed them to live vicariously through the rich and free. I personally could not care less about what was going on with another prisoner because that information brought me no closer to freedom, but that did not mean that others weren't concerned with what was going on with me. As soon as the other 18 prisoners and I left our parole hearings in Building 61, rumors began. It was said that at least 12 of us were successful at obtaining parole. Who started this rumor was unknown to me. None of us knew the outcome of our hearing that soon and even though I knew that it was improbable for anyone to know the decisions yet, I was tempted to give some credence to the rumor. I wanted it to be true and wanted to be one of the 12 who were granted parole. But I knew that it would not be that easy. The rumors made the wait for my decision that much harder.

It would be a few days before I received my decision about parole. When I couldn't paint or concentrate enough to read, I just lay on my bed thinking. Things were going to change one way or another. Either I would win my freedom or worse, the Parole Commissioners would add another two years to my sentence and I would still be trapped inside a cage that I refused to get used to.

Friday arrived. I had to wait until 2:30 p.m. for the prison's Law Library to open so I could pick up my parole decision. From 8:00 a.m. until 2:30 p.m., prison gossip clashed with prisoner inquiries of who won parole and who didn't. This was an explosive combination. Fellow prisoners would become thirsty to know your fate as if your parole decision somehow affected them as well. A silent camaraderie seemed to exist around parole decision time. Some of the concern came from prisoners who were coming up for parole soon and wanted some hope. Others were never getting out of prison alive, or no time soon, so witnessing a fellow prisoner be released was their brief moment to taste the idea of freedom once more.

But outside of that very strange kinship there were the institutionalized leeches who were looking to see what possessions they could get their hands on once a prisoner made parole. These guys were forever looking to make their prison stay as comfortable as possible, even if that meant hoarding property and placing unnecessary value on things that really did not matter. A more comfortable stay in prison was their freedom and life on the outside was just trouble for them. They would rather see a seasoned prisoner leave and his bed be opened up for a new jack prisoner they could possibly exploit in some way than for a prisoner not to be released and they get nothing out of the deal. I stayed far away from those characters because they were like the crack and heroin users around my old home, or the Black men who I would always tell myself I would never be like because they were doing nothing with themselves other than stagnating on street corners. These prisoners were now stagnating in their cellblocks with no desire for something greater than a used pair of sneakers or some extra commissary items.

Now 2:30 arrived and I was doing everything to avoid picking up my decision from the law library. It was a long walk from my housing unit and I expected that the walk there would not be a lonely one with all the other prisoners curious to know parole decisions. Parole hearings were a big deal in prison and everyone wanted to know how the Parole Commissioners thought, as if the granting of freedom for at least one or two of us was hope for all the others. So 2:30 came and I hesitated and avoided the Law Library altogether. I decided to wait until 6 p.m. instead.

"On the evening recreation and programs!" the C.O. yelled into the dormitory. It was now about time to pick up my decision. I could do no more to avoid this moment. What was going to be was going to be and I would have to deal with it either way. I was hoping for the best but after years inside the beast, I was prepared for the worst and had already given myself the necessary pep talk to get me through another two years in prison. It was not going to be easy. I still had not conditioned myself to find prison a comfortable place to sleep, let alone to exist in. Maybe, just maybe, the Parole Commissioners actually granted me freedom and I would soon enough be reunited with my family. It was a stretching of hope, because even I knew that the current political climate was tough on violent felony offenders and the Governor had made it clear that he was against ever releasing violent prisoners back into their communities.

My worst fear became my fate – the answer was NO. Parole denied.

CHAPTER 3

THE VALLEY AND GANG BANGING

IT WAS not until I reached the age of 16 and was living at the Harlem Valley Secure Center that I discovered myself within an historical context and learned to view history and politics in relationship to my own life and experience. Before this, there was no context to my life. I had existed inside a vacuum and I hadn't done much thinking about the larger world around me to connect it with my own life. Newburgh was the only world I had known. Everything I understood about the world came from experiences and observations on my block. It was limited but I wasn't dead. I had learned not to trust anyone and had learned how dangerous the world actually was, all from the view of my block. But after I was sentenced to nine years to life and sent off to serve my jail time in a juvenile prison for murder, I was in a different world, a strange other world, the place where O.G.'s in my neighborhood were sent when they were bagged for their crimes. O.G.'s were literally "original gangsters," but in street talk they were older men who had the street eloquence to survive life in the ghetto and maybe offer some priceless wisdom to the youth coming up behind them. This other world of chains and shackles, guards and uniforms, and hundreds of young Black males all housed together away from the free world, gave me a strong motivation to want to know what was really going on and what I got myself caught up in. I wanted to explore my self-identity because I knew that I had to be more than just another young Black male doing hard time.

I got placed in by far one of the worst New York State juvenile prison blocks, Unit G, which housed the most violent youthful offenders from all over New York City and upstate New York. There was not one teenager in the unit who was convicted of anything less than armed robbery or homicide. Unit G housed about 25 young men, all of whom were ideologically divided by the gang that they were members of.

Because of the gang activity that was happening down at Rikers Island, and the New York Bloods having their start in the prison system just three years before my incarceration, there were more Bloods than any other gang in the unit. Crips and Latin Kings, although outnumbered, still made their presence known and were equally fearless. They all were at odds with one another so Unit G was always on and popping with gang brawls. Living in Unit G meant that you had to be affiliated with one of these gangs if you wanted to survive. Most juveniles didn't possess the kind of personality that could afford them neutrality and survival. It wasn't that way in the streets and it certainly wasn't that way in lockup.

My first few seconds after arriving in Unit G were going to determine where I would stand among all the other youth. When I got to the unit, after being processed and identified in the prison's receiving room, everyone was already locked into their rooms. And even though I could not see the faces locked behind their doors, their cacophonous screams and taunts made it clear that they were present and hungry for new blood. They were wolves and I happened to be the new jack that their rage and juvenile testosterone wanted to feast upon. But since I was just given a life sentence and had to be there for a while, my becoming a victim of any sort was not how I planned on doing my time.

As I was being lead to my new room to get locked in, the other youth already in their rooms were engaged in conversation. Some were rapping and using their doors as drums to mimic hip hop beats. And then out of nowhere, several Bloods all in unison began to sing out their roll call. "P-E-A-C-E A-L-M-I-G-H-T-Y!" the voice of one Blood yelled and the others chimed in fluidly, "PEACE BLOOOOD!" That was the first time I had witnessed a call and response. Of course I had no understanding of context at that time but no doubt about it, their roll call was as tribal African or indigenous as it could possibly get. There was a power in their voice and a unity that was beyond gang affiliation and colored bandanas. They were a tribe or had the potential to create a solidarity rooted in numbers and common experience. The only message they all understood was that numbers meant a more dominant presence and a greater threat of violence against others.

When I got to my cell, the staff member escorting me closed the door behind me and locked it. I was in Harlem Valley now and there was no escaping. It was time to get myself prepared for the unknown. One of the first things I remember doing was thoroughly checking my room for any weapons that may have been stashed by a previous occupant, and I made sure that I had enough space around me to move about in case I had to fight in my first few days on the unit. Coming from the streets where survival was first priority in a waking man's agenda, I had learned to study my environment and to read people inside out. The streets had bred no trust of other people so it was easy to think that all the other young men around me assumed that I was just as much a threat as they were. I would later realize how emotionally draining and psychologically unhealthy it was to live among others who resembled you in more ways than the differences that separated us, and still not be able to trust one another. But at 15 and 16 years old, life wasn't very deep. It was really all about fun and games and in between extreme violence and making sure that you didn't become the next victim. I was the new kid in Unit G and all eyes were already locked on me to see where I stood and what position I was going to play within the social order that existed among Unit G's young gangbangers.

CHAPTER 4

REAGAN, CRACK DEALS & ART

GANGS WERE and still are an everyday reality for young people in Newburgh. Gang life came with an attitude, language, and a code of conduct that fuels more than any other force the underground black markets of street commerce and culture. Deep poverty and inner-city blues are ripe ingredients for the formation of street cliques. In the 1980s and 1990s, Newburgh was already on the map as one of America's toughest cities to live in. Gang life was seizing almost every street corner in the city. The Ave Boys, Nation Wide, and Posse were some of the largest homegrown gangs in the city during the 1980s. These gangs were mostly made up of youth who all went to the same school or who lived on the same block. Members of these gangs viewed one another as family and all outsiders as enemies. These gangs were locally based and didn't have national aspirations so their criminal pursuits were not as lofty as more popular gangs today such as the Bloods and Crips.

In the 1980s two tragedies would befall Black urban America. The first tragedy began with the election of Ronald Reagan to the U.S. presidency in 1980, and the second was when the Black community got introduced to crack-cocaine. Neither crack nor Reagan were good for Black people. With Reagan as President, the executive branch of the government ceased to support expanded Civil Rights that protected the disenfranchised of America, namely the poor and Black. Reagan's administration also sought to reduce welfare programs and it staffed key agencies and the federal judiciary with opponents of Affirmative Action – an Act designed to prevent racial discrimination in college admissions and hiring.

Ronald Reagan's defeat of Jimmy Carter, the Democratic Presidential candidate, had negative symbolic implications for Black America. To many poor Blacks, Reagan symbolized the emergence of the "New Right" as the dominant force in American politics. People simply did not believe that Reagan had their best interests at heart. He certainly did not speak about improving their social and economic conditions without erasing them as Urban Renewal did in the 1960s.

One of the New Right's key goals was to reverse the growth of social welfare programs created during and after the New Deal. From 1981 to 1993, Reagan and his Republican successor George Bush, cut federal grants to cities in half and terminated programs crucial to the stability of many inner-city families. Reagan also advanced the infamous "trickle-down" theory of economics. He believed that if the financial position of the wealthiest Americans improved, their increased prosperity would percolate down through the middle and working classes to the poor. This notion was proved false. Reagan's politics left urban America more marginalized and disenfranchised. With the eradication of social programs that taught urban Blacks vocational trades and other educational skills, and with weakened safety nets for the urban poor, Newburgh's inner city became an open target for new black markets and new predators.

Sometime between 1984 and 1986, crack cocaine hit the streets in my community. All it took was a few years for crack to transform Newburgh's inner city into a slum. First the people went, and then the city went. Downtown Newburgh literally morphed into a City of the Walking Dead. Crack robbed people of their souls. It destroyed people psychologically, emotionally and physically and it deteriorated family relationships. The devastation of that drug was all around us. My brothers and I would play outside on the street or in parks and constantly dribble our basketball over empty crack vials and broken pipe stems.

Our first apartment in the city that I recall was on Broadway. Broadway was a long strip that extended from west to east, right through the middle of the city, from Route 17K all the way down to the Hudson River. And we lived dead center in all of the bad action. At night Broadway would be draped with a curtain of street lights that ran up and down both sides of the street. At night, when I was as young as five years old, I would stare out my bedroom window and watch the street transform into a spectacle of flowing bodies, cars, and exchanges of laughter and poison. I would look out in awe at a world that was magically intertwined with Black suffering and Black attempts to find meaning in a concrete jungle.

Gangs ruled during the night and did their business with the addicts and prostitutes who could be seen strolling up and down Broadway. I could hear rap music played from portable radios and car stereos. That was the first time I actually heard rap music. The sound was magnetic, as it seemed to draw the entire night scene together into a beautiful mosaic – block parties, loud laughter echoing through the air, sparkling gold chains swinging from the necks of young Black and brown bodies. That world of bold color and chaotic beauty was an intense palette. Then at the apex of my amusement would quickly come a commotion, then a brawl. And then loud shots like July 4th would ring out, without dazzling fireworks painting the dark sky. Women would scream and silhouettes would scatter in opposite directions. A nameless person would be lying in his own pool of blood and I would hear police sirens lamenting in the distance. I would dart back away from the window and fearfully hide myself under the bed sheets and fall asleep.

Being a spectator of that chaotic world and having been introduced to the myriad of colors beneath my window is probably what pushed me towards art. I wanted to recreate what I was witnessing to understand things and their purpose, especially since I couldn't be a part of them outside directly. My mother said I was four years old when I began to scribble murals on her kitchen walls.

I found art or rather art found me. No one in my family before me had been an artist. So whether it was a God-given talent or born out of a necessity to make sense of the community around me, art became a language that I could actually work with and feel comfortable using. To begin with, there wasn't a whole lot of communication happening inside my house, and if so the language was confined to the literal daily experiences of my mother and my eldest sisters. My mother had suffered an ear infection as a child that caused her deafness and limited what she communicated, and my dad had a heavy Caribbean tongue that sometimes sounded like mumbo jumbo to me. Because of this early deprivation of language, I forced myself to imitate the sounds and images that came from outside our home by committing lines and shapes to paper methodically until I sketched my own very juvenile relationship to everything outside. I didn't know that what I was doing was called art. In the beginning it was just a way for me to express my fondness for the unknown outside of my bedroom window. It was how I could become one with the beautiful madness of the street without ever having to step outside into it. My art was personal, spiritual in a sense. It was a space of true peace, a comfort zone even, that would make more sense to me than the arguing and shouting that my parents and the strangers below me in the street engaged in frequently. Then someone came along and gave it a name and I became a young artist.

Art would be part of my childhood and it was always intertwined with everything else that was going on in my life. My love for art always followed any juvenile delinquency that I and my friends got into. The gangbanging and the running from marked and unmarked police cars through back alleys because my friends and I were spray-painting graffiti on abandoned buildings, was later sketched in one of my drawing pads. Graffiti drawings that read "Fuck 12" or full colored intricate pieces that screamed our crew name, were my way of being rebellious and still being true to my art. When I became a little older I was introduced to photography and the work of the late photographer Gordon Parks. His style of photography I fell in love with instantly and was absolutely inspired by it. Like Parks, I would one day use a camera as a weapon to tell truth to power and to humanize an inner city section of America that was systemically and aesthetically devoid of beauty.

CHAPTER 5

LOSING MY SUPERMAN FATHER

MEMORIES ESCAPE me whenever I think about my Dad. As my mother explained it, my father chose the streets over his own family. His decision not to be there was easy when the consumption of drugs and other women became part of his life. My mother had no tolerance for any of his bad habits so she put him out of the house. I was about eight years old when Dad last lived with us. So I remember him vaguely and recall only his tall posture, chiseled features, and his patois speaking voice scolding my two younger brothers and me for playing too loudly throughout the house. My Dad was a strict man who ruled with an iron fist. As the man of the household, his way was the only way. My mother said it had come from his patriarchal driven West Indian background – men ruled and women followed. Dad was born on the small Caribbean island of Trinidad and Tobago in 1942, as World War II began. Because of wretched poverty and lack of opportunity on the island, my father and his parents emigrated from Trinidad while my dad was in his teens. They arrived in the United States sometime in the late 1950s. They ended up in Louisville, Kentucky, and my dad enlisted in the U.S. Army in 1958 when he was 17 years old. Joining the Army back then was the easiest way for a Black man to avoid the crudest forms of racism practiced in civilian life, and a free way to travel the country and the world. Once my father joined the army, he never looked back to his previous life and barely stayed in contact with his parents and siblings.

After the Vietnam War, my father was discharged from the Army in 1975 and began working entry-level jobs throughout the country, traveling by train from state to state until he made his way to Newburgh, New York, around 1977 or 1978. There he met my mother and gave her three sons. He was there for the first eight years and according to accounts from my sisters, he was a good father and provider and protected us while he was around. But then destructive drugs hit Newburgh metaphorically in the same way that the atomic bomb hit Nagasaki and Hiroshima in Japan – if drugs weren't the bomb itself then they were the radiation afterwards that ripped through America's cities, affecting the Black community badly in many ways.

Black fathers either became users or dealers because the drug culture had become a new economy for a lot of Black men, and crack was a high that caught on fast and its addiction was hard to kick. But the backlash of selling crack came with harsh penalties that sent an overwhelming number of Black men to prison for decades and even life due to the national War on Drugs Policy that deliberately targeted urban Black communities. Those policies and crack itself destroyed the Black family and took fathers out of the home. My father was never incarcerated but he was no exception from the many missing Black fathers. When my dad left us, there was no forewarning or any discussion before or after. Not a word of goodbye from him. He just disappeared and we all had to deal with his absence. My mother became a single mom overnight and we all had to learn to fend for ourselves quickly. The normalcy of it all still disturbs me. The silence and the untreated and unrecognized trauma of losing someone as important as a father, under any circumstances, pains me deeply to this day. Families and children were expected to just carry on as if fathers were not supposed to be part of the family dynamic. Only one of my friends still had his dad living at home. But otherwise, father figures were an uncommon thing for me growing up.

With no father at home to teach me how to become a man, I was destined for childhood rebellion that would either get me killed or incarcerated. At one point my mother tried to substitute the absence of my father with images and stories of Black men who were great in her own childhood. All throughout the house hung crucifixes of Black men who were slain for their political beliefs. Mother had portraits of Dr. Martin Luther King, Jr. and Malcolm X decorating the walls in the living room. I suppose she was hoping that their images would in some way summon their spirits into our household. And even if Martin and Malcolm were not to mean anything to me and my brothers in my dad's absence, I clearly remember other Black men reminding me of Martin and Malcolm's tragic death. The summoning of their spirits never happened of course, but I was seeing more of Malcolm and Martin and other lesser-known radicals of my race than my own father. And not even their presence could contain my rambunctious hormones and my adolescent frustrations that were both throwing me into rough manhood where I felt the need to always speak my mind. Speaking my mind was getting me in trouble with my mom and it was getting me in trouble at school.

By the fifth grade, I was labeled a troublemaker by my teacher for not pledging allegiance to the American flag. The class was expected to stand up and pledge every morning and I was waiting for the right moment to let the teacher know that I was refusing to do so. I wasn't anti-America. I was cynical and fatherless. And I paid attention to the contradictions of American history. Every morning before classes would begin, the school's principal would get on the intercom asking everyone to stand and pledge their allegiance to the flag. One day I was going to rebel against the principal's order by remaining in my seat.

Once all of the hallways were clear of students and classrooms filled, the intercom came on with the same voice every day instructing students to stand. One day I didn't stand and in fact I sat through the entire pledge. My classmates chuckled at me without them being caught by the teacher. They figured I was being a class clown but I knew better. I knew what I was doing. The teacher, Mrs. Rollins, immediately spotted me and walked over to ask me to step into the hallway. She wanted to know why I didn't stand and by the tone of her voice she was more concerned about my random act of rebellion than actually hearing my pre-teen opinions on American politics. I don't recall what amateur radical speech I must have given her. My real issue was that I was angry. I was angry that my dad wasn't around and I needed someone to blame. Not knowing how to articulate that pain, I was too intelligent to be a class clown. So instead I became a classroom rebel. It was easier to defy authority than to get any answers about why my father was nowhere to be found. My defiance would grow like a cancer because my mother could not contain me at home and my teachers could not contain me at school.

No one was even attempting to respond to the real reason for my silent cries. So I hid my pain behind my classroom defiance and used every opportunity I found to tell Mrs. Rollins that the American flag didn't mean anything to me other than a symbol of the divide between my own neighborhood and the America that was idealized by Mrs. Rollins and other teachers. That idealized America, I never got to experience. Where was "freedom" on my neighborhood block? Where was my father and the fathers of all of my friends? Why was my friend's mom strung out on crack? As I saw things, the young guys around me carried guns in the same manner as rebels in South Africa or Syria do. The cops harassed us and monitored us every hour of the day as if we were all criminals. Drugs, violence and poverty turned my neighborhood into a war zone.

My young eyes did not see "liberty and justice for all."

So I often spoke my mind and disrupted the class and was often sent to the principal's office. After a while, Mrs. Rollins stopped sending me to the principal's office altogether and never again demanded that I stand for the pledge. I eventually outgrew disrupting her classroom as the school year progressed. But I was still living with all of this pent up pain stemming from all the unanswered questions about my missing father. The older I became, the more prone I became to falling victim of my poisonous neighborhood. I needed my father to be my hero.

I needed him to throw on his cape and to prove that he was my superman. But my superman never came home.

CHAPTER 6

AN IRISH ACTIVIST FOR HOUSING

THE YEAR 1985 was a year full of hell for the city of Newburgh. There were random fires in Black and Latino homes all throughout the city. Newburgh was another South Bronx, reminiscent of the 1970s era when many of the poor parts of the Bronx were burning down. The arsonists were never known but the fires were always deemed suspicious and deliberate. Families were becoming homeless one after another, but city officials took no action as the inner city was burning down. This unconcerned attitude quickly made Newburgh's poor residents distrust the white establishment and many Blacks began to blame the Fire Chief and Mayor for the fires. So many properties were being destroyed and so many families were being uprooted from the neighborhood that folks considered these burnings an obvious part of a program sanctioned by city officials who conspired with slumlords. It was reported that while one fire was bringing an apartment down to ruins, the white fire chief yelled to the other firemen, "Clean these bastards out!"

Eventually Black and Latino families began to have conversations about the problems facing their community. Community organizing began to take root when a group of local nuns and activists agreed to put Newburgh's issues on the table. At the helm of the organizing was a young white female attorney named Clare Overlander.

Clare, who would later become a life-long friend of my family, was a serious fighter for poor people, and a fiery attorney who invigorated the marginalized and impoverished people of Newburgh with her radical ideas and action. I was one of the youngest people at the organizing meetings, always tucked under my mother's arm and waiting to burst from her body whenever the meeting would be adjourned for donuts and apple cider. These meetings were always packed with women. Men from the community were hardly ever present. They weren't in the household. They weren't in church. And they weren't organizing in the streets. They were missing in action, either incarcerated or strung out on drugs. It was the women of Newburgh who were fighting to make a difference, Black and Latino and compassionate white women. In one of many conversations that we would share, Clare talked about her early life and how she had become involved in social activism.

Clare's parents, both Irish immigrants, would regularly have conversations with her about the struggles of Irish immigrants in this country. In many ways Clare likened the Irish struggle for assimilation to the American Black struggle. They were both minority groups widely rejected by the dominant culture.

Raised in the Hell's Kitchen section of New York City, her parents worked endless days and nights to survive mainstream America which possessed another set of racist attitudes toward European immigrants. Hearing her parents' story and growing up in that social climate of discrimination gave her a personal understanding and relationship to those at the bottom of society and she felt a need to fight for them.

Clare was taught to be anti-racist, so during her school years she was always attracted to and made friends with students of color. Multicultural students she believed brought diversity to her friendships and taught her things about different groups that her own white skin prevented her from knowing. Clare was well aware of her white privilege and understood how that privilege was rooted in Eurocentrism, which blinded whites from seeing the humanity of others.

Many whites believed that Blacks did not or should not have a meaningful political or legal status in America. White anger toward Black progress only increased in American society. Racial violence permeated Black urban life in the most pervasive form, police brutality. It was these conditions that led Black self-defense groups like the Black Panther Party to liken their neighborhoods to exploited colonies kept in poverty by repressive white political and economic institutions.

Each summer between 1965 and 1969, Black despair flared into urban rebellion beginning with the Watts rebellion of 1965 in Los Angeles, followed by Newark and then Detroit. It was this atmosphere, along with the assassinations of three of their heroes, President John Kennedy, Dr. Martin Luther King Jr., and Robert Kennedy, that gave birth to Clare's social consciousness.

Clare left Newton, Massachusetts, to teach in New York State high schools before attending law school to study environmental law in Brooklyn. She was admitted to the Bar in 1981.

In the early 1980s, Clare was introduced to a group of Catholic nuns in Baltimore who frequently did missionary work in Nicaragua. One of these nuns was Sister Maria Theresa Bourbon, a long time Newburgh resident who brought Clare to Newburgh to do some legal work within our community.

After the criminal burning of homes in Newburgh's inner city in 1985, someone insisted that the fire victims find an attorney. Through the collective networking of Newburgh's inner city residents and some concerned outsiders, the organization NUJH (Neighbors United for Justice in Housing) was formed in 1986 and Clare became the attorney representing several of the families which were displaced by the fires.

The platform of NUJH was clear and explicit. NUJH aimed to create safe, decent and affordable housing with and for those made poor in the inner city. With Newburgh's inner-city being the second poorest district in New York State and having over 80% of its people below the national poverty income level, NUJH's objective was not only pragmatic but desperately needed. NUJH didn't last long but it was effective while it was active. It provided several homes for the poor of Newburgh, making a few poor families homeowners.

NUJH attempted several meetings with City Hall officials, but officials made it clear that there would be no economic development to contribute to the health of the city's poor residents. This official turning of their back policy compounded the even more devastating flow of the crack epidemic during the 1980s and 1990s that exacerbated the already extremely high poverty levels and the homeless crisis in the city. NUJH was forced to take action in the only manner that would get the city's response. They staged a sit-in at City Hall, and made the mayor acknowledge their grievances. One of their demands was that the City sell to NUJH abandoned and dilapidated buildings for $2,500 each that would be used to house first-time homeowners, all of whom were poor and would otherwise never have the opportunity to own property. The city conceded. NUJH won that battle.

Eventually internal conflicts and damaging ideological struggles forced Clare Overlander to resign from NUJH in 1989. NUJH dismembered in the mid-1990s, leaving a troubled city and its minority groups with no leadership or protection against corrupt and apathetic city government.

In 1996 Clare left Newburgh to do human rights work in Germany. Some years later, she returned to the United States to attend Yale University, where she received a Masters in Divinity and worked as a pastor in a church in Massachusetts.

Newburgh was an overwhelmingly depressed city. Many good people just left rather than staying and getting worn out. I was too young at 15 to just pack my things and leave so I had to deal with whatever troubles came my way. I had no idea that the year 1996 was going to be so overwhelming that I would be trapped in major trouble that would begin a new chapter of struggles in my life.

CHAPTER 7

THE BLACK BUDDHA

THE YOUTH Counselors I encountered at the Harlem Valley Secure Center, for those six years of my juvenile detention, helped to nourish and develop racial pride in me. The majority of the staff were Black and the majority of the incarcerated youth were also Black. So the Valley was a place of tough love and the counselors there understood first hand where we came from and what we needed. It was here that I started to gain a social consciousness rooted in Afrocentricity and around Indigenous culture. Before then I didn't have much cultural awareness at all. I didn't see being Black as cultural or tied to a broader cultural context. The Black American, according to how it was taught to me in my early education, was not particularly African and specifically not related to anything indigenous. The Black American began as an uncouth slave who could become Americanized only through chains and plantation torture, but because of permanent Black skin a Black American was not fully American and indeed a perpetual target of American racism. That was the limit of Black American history offered to me by my early educators. I knew that I was Black and that I had come from a screwed up place full of Black families struggling daily to survive, where white cops were constantly on the prowl to make our lives much more difficult. Being

Black was a badge of shame. Before my cultural awakening, Blacks seemed inferior to whites.

Schools had taught us that the history of Black Americans began in 1619 on the first slave plantation in America, and a few centuries later we were free to roam the ghettos of contemporary society. They never taught us about Black African history, Black leaders, Black inventors and Black achievements before or after slavery. So I, like every other Black youth, took it that we were just a race of Niggas stuck in America and hated by white authority.

It was part of New York State prison protocol that counselors refrain from getting too involved with the residents. Their job was only to supervise the residents and to ensure safety while the detained youth did their prison sentences. After all, most of us were sentenced as adults, serving time for serious crimes and almost all of us still had gang affiliations and were menaces even in confinement. But that didn't stop many of the counselors from establishing close relations with residents and bringing in literature that was restricted by prison policy. I never quite understood why institutions would have a ban on Black literature that could serve Black youth and educate them in ways that public schools obviously failed. Because I was a resident who wasn't interested in fighting every day, counselors gravitated towards me and respected my maturity. I was always reading books and writing in my journal so it was just a matter of time before some staff would take a liking to me and would start introducing me to Black literature.

Fred Livingston was one of the first Black youth counselors with whom I established a student-educator relationship. We called him the Buddha because he was a short pudgy man with a protruding stomach who suffered from sleep apnea. Because of this condition he would often fall asleep on the job and we always got a kick out of a prison guard falling asleep while in charge of monitoring criminals. Buddha prided himself in having a black belt in martial arts and claimed that he could kick any one of our asses, if we chose to try him.

Most of us doubted him. But we all respected him so no one ever tried to fight with him.

How I came to meet Buddha I could never forget. It was during my first week at the Valley. I was in the intake area getting processed by one of the facility counselors who would assign me a living unit and class. By the time I was escorted to my class, the class was already in session and instead of the Norwegian teacher, it was Buddha putting a rowdy class in line and lecturing to the Black and Latino residents on the subject of Black History. When I walked into the classroom and witnessed a room of teenagers captivated by this fat-bellied Black man, I knew there was something powerful about him, that he could command the attention of a classroom of crazy youth. He had an eloquence and street savvy in his speech. He was making everything plain and simple, connecting dots and telling the classroom that we all were part of a much bigger scheme that we were now too blind to see.

Buddha was the first Black person I met who knew Black History that wasn't all negative and victimizing. On the contrary, Buddha walked us through thousands of years of ancient African kingdoms and the technologies they had invented before any European had made a mark on human history. Buddha wasn't afraid to give it up raw and uncut, unlike all of my elementary and middle school teachers who never once touched the subject of Black History. Buddha spoke candidly about things that we had never imagined could be possible and he verified everything with books to back up what he was speaking to us about. His storytelling was magic and everyone in the classroom sat quiet. Even the white teacher was attentive and mesmerized by his depth of never- before-told historical accounts of Black achievement. He was elevating all of us and subconsciously moving some of us to a center of Black love that was before empty and shrouded in hate. I personally was deeply interested in what he was talking about and wanted to hear more of what he had to say.

It was never a matter of me hating school. I hated what my early teachers taught. I felt unrelated to everything about the classroom. Whenever I attempted to ask questions, teachers always regarded me as a rabble-rouser, so my questions were never answered. We were expected to just sit there and allow the teacher to deposit information in our heads without questioning it. I was too inquisitive not to be the kind of student who asked questions. I was definitely a seeker of knowledge even if I didn't know what it was that I was searching for. But somehow whatever it was that I was searching for lead me to the Valley where I would grow on so many levels. And Buddha was one of the first good teachers on my journey of self-discovery.

Admittedly I thought I was a pretty sharp kid and believed that I already had many of the answers to life, like most kids my age. One day I made the mistake of trying to impose what I thought I knew onto Buddha as he sat at his desk in the counselors' office. A few books under my belt had me thinking that I was a Black history expert and that I could actually debate with a man like Buddha. I was a novice in Black literature and started off reading militant and Black Nationalist works because writers like Malcolm X and people like Stokely Carmichael (aka Kwame Ture) spoke to my angst and rage. Emotionally and in my warped imagination, I believed the revolution was going to happen any day now and I was going to fight my way out of this juvenile prison and back into the streets to wage war against the white man and specifically against the white judge who showed no leniency to me. Fortunately, cultured individuals like Buddha humbled me fast because I was letting 1960s Black militant speeches get into my head. He was sitting in the office as I approached to build with him on some of the things that I was reading. I had no idea that I was in for a humbling experience.

It was one thing to learn from him, but I was also interested in debating with Buddha to validate my own confidence. I remember baiting him with a frivolous question, in hopes that he would respond and be forced to argue with me. But Buddha saw exactly what I was doing a mile away. He swiftly answered my first question and as soon as I tried to throw another question at him, he quickly slapped me across my lips and told me to shut up. Buddha wasn't angry. He was teaching me a lesson about talking so much that I failed to hear others talk. I was stunned by the fact that he had the nerve to put his hands on me. Strangely, Buddha comforted me by saying that he could see my soul through my eyes. "I know your every thought, boy!" he said. I just stood there with a stinging mouth, ready to take in his wisdom. "How about you shut up, stop speaking and just listen! The more you talk, the less you learn!" he would say. After getting a dose of both his karate and his wisdom all in one, listening is what I did. Buddha began to share his knowledge with me because I was humble enough to receive it. I was amazed that one person could retain that much wealth of information about the Black race and its true history.

It seemed like Buddha knew everything under the sun. He talked about ancient Black History and showed me where Africa was mentioned in the Bible. He knew a lot more about Christianity than the white Jesus my mother called upon in her worried moments. We talked about Black organizations and Black figures who had emerged in the early 20th Century. We also talked about Indigenous spirituality, numerology and astrology, how Egypt was once Black and how powerful African Kingdoms had existed right up to the beginning of the Trans-Atlantic Slave Trade. Buddha was astonishing with his knowledge. He even knew about Free Masonry and the Black Masons known as Prince Hall Free Masons. I learned that it was a Black man by the name of Benjamin Banneker who helped design Washington, DC, and was the first African-American to write an Almanac. I truly enjoyed learning from Buddha. He was one of the first educators who transformed prison into a place of higher learning. I remembered Malcolm X writing that prison was the second best place in America to get a higher education.

As time went on I began to see less and less of Buddha. He was not working my housing unit as much and was not coming to work as regularly as he had before. At times he would show up to work for maybe a week every three or four months. Then all of a sudden he didn't show up at all. I would later learn that Buddha's rotund physique and constant tiredness had to do with his health problems. Eventually he would never return to the Valley. I still had many years to go in my stay in the Valley and as much as I would miss Buddha, he had given me enough Black History to inspire my quest for self-knowledge and Black dignity.

It didn't take long for the revelation that I was incarcerated inside the Belly of the Beast. The Beast was not just my own physical confinement. It was also my attitude and the wrong information that I had picked up from the streets. The digestion of backward thinking turned my brain into dead matter and I was my own worst enemy. We all were. Every single youth around me, in the Valley, we were all our own worst enemies. But I wanted to be free. I wanted to become mentally free. I always felt this way. Even when I was a kid in the streets I had this same yearning, something great felt missing from my life and that void was becoming bigger each day. Knowledge of self, a phrase and methodology that was preached by the Black Muslim movement, but certainly not limited to it, was the only philosophical key that could free my mind from the shackles of ignorance that still controlled my brain a century after the physical slavery of my ancestors had ended in America.

Youth Counselors Mr. Mack and Mr. Deyo were two people who soon replaced Buddha. Mr. Mack was a jovial Black man originally from Chicago who reminded me of the late great Black comedians Robin Harris and Bernie Mack, and who often mimicked their famous speech patterns and jokes to get us all laughing. Mr. Mack was full of personality and used comedy as part of his way of reaching us young men. Like several other counselors, Mack didn't respect the prison policy of not bringing in books for the residents. He would say that we were criminals but not animals. We needed education more than we needed salvation. He and Mr. Deyo were sneaking in books for me and a handful of others every time they came to work. Education was stripping away my mental chains one by one, every time I absorbed new books. I was feeling less like a prisoner and more like how a college student felt surrounded by academia.

In the ghetto we were self-absorbed and mostly consumed with the necessity of survival that often pitted us against one another. The idea of us working together as a Black community died when crack took over. So Black love and loving myself was a new construct that I had to learn. Mr. Mack was bringing me works by historians such as John G. Jackson, Cheikh Anta Diop, John Henrick Clarke, J.A. Rogers, and Yosef Ben-Jochannan. Mr. Deyo was the first Five-Percenter I had met. A Five-Percenter or *The God,* a more commonly accepted term, was a member of a quasi-Islamic cultural group mostly known for working toward the development and achievement of inner city Black youth. The Fiver-Percenters were also respectfully known as the Nation of Gods and Earths. This organization was my first introduction to Black cosmology which was one of several vital pillars of an authentic Black place within time and space. Through the teachings of the Nation, Mr. Deyo told me that as a Black man I was the original man and a direct descendant of God, because the earliest human fossils discovered were that of a Black woman found in Africa. The list of Black writers was abundant and the information I was learning was blowing me away. It was opening my eyes and I was always craving for more. I was convinced that I had been lied to in the public schools I had attended. My teachers had lied to me, some of whom were Black themselves, all part of a conspiracy I believed to keep Black inner-city youth grossly ignorant of their true racial and historical identity. If Black kids weren't afforded the opportunity to love themselves by learning about the rich history of African and of Black contributions to the world, then they would surely learn to hate themselves and hate their own kind as they absorb and internalize the dominance of whiteness that prevailed in public education.

I soon fell in love with the words and the illustrations of these Black authors. Romanticism or not, I was becoming a voracious reader of Black literature and turned my little room in the Valley into a library of Black excellence. One author after another was feeding and expanding my consciousness. I finally grew in love with the skin that I was in. This new found knowledge taught me that I could be greater than a drug dealer or gangster. And for the first time the narrative wasn't that people who looked like me were only addicts and killers of other Blacks. We were more than a bunch of Niggas running from and being shot down by the police. How did I ever come to accept such a negative perspective, I would wonder?

History had placed me in pre-Columbus Spain where Black Moors had ruled for over 700 years. Dark skinned people were the architects of the pyramids and built the earliest civilizations, invented writing, the calendar, performed the first surgeries, erected grand lodges and libraries of higher learning throughout the Middle East and Africa. We were even in the Americas before Europeans ventured the seas in the 15th Century. This can be seen in the massive Olmec heads with distinct African features discovered in South America. We were a great people who fell because of wars, conflict and slavery. We were not just the slave experience. We were much more than that. But systemic racism and white supremacy denied us this truth and erased us from Western and other World civilizations. These Black authors allowed me to see for the first time how great my racial lineage actually was. Beyond the personal pain and frustration of being reduced to a badge of shame and feeling rejected by the white world, I was realizing the devastation of my own neighborhood. My Black community was a victim of this white washing of history.

CHAPTER 8

DADDY ISSUES

MY MOTHER was the second youngest of her five siblings born to my grandparents, Daniel and Annabelle Allen. Her baby sister Juanita had died from pneumonia only months after being born. They lived and grew up in a time and place where the residue of slavery and racial segregation was still fresh in the memory of Black folk, and still the culture of the Segregated South. My mother was born in the 1940s, after the Great Depression and during the Jim Crow era when depressing and dehumanizing Black Codes were still publicly practiced. Black people had it hard back then. Times are still hard, and new generations face new challenges, but there are social service resources available today that weren't available during my mother's era. My mother and her generation survived their hard times with a solidarity and steadfastness that is widely missing from my own generation. They stood together, stuck together, fought and survived together.

My generation lost that sense of solidarity over time. Nowadays it is common to hear young people express a "gang against gang" mindset that is rooted in a divide and conquer trap. We are sectarian and greatly selfish and this has us constantly pitted against one another. Bad enough that cops already kill us and Klansmen once hunted us down and lynched us. In my mother's generation they found ways to survive peacefully and without becoming creators of their own destruction. The social ills of the past continue to show their ugly heads today but the problems in the streets are exacerbated by the overwhelming presence of drugs and illegal firearms among young people. Guns in the hands of youth automatically intensify the conflict. It is the means by which Black youth take each other out one by one.

Growing up I thought of my mother as a woman of tremendous strength. She had made it through the forties, the fifties, the sixties, the seventies, and still had enough strength to care for her six children alone. She was raising all of us by herself. I didn't understand why but Black fathers never stuck around long enough to co-parent, leaving mothers struggling to feed a whole bunch of hungry mouths. My mother was a survivalist. Her experience in the South taught her how to make ends meet and how to keep her head above water. We were indeed poor growing up but mother was clever at hiding that. My entire neighborhood was poor so we all shared identical problems. In fact I think we all equated being Black with being equally poor and, of course, whites had to be wealthy because they didn't live among us but in another world.

We always had food on the table and a roof above our heads but those things didn't compensate for the absence of my father. We all needed him. His absence was like a blistering wound that would not heal. No one ever talked about him returning so eventually that wound would become callous. But underneath that callous I was sure that my mother was still hurt along with her children. My mother always found ways to cope. Everything was manageable for her as long as I didn't become a teenager. Once I hit my teens, there was no way she could raise me from boy to man, let alone control me. Adolescence meant acting out and being defiant in a misdirected attempt to affirm my maleness in the absence of a real man to guide me in the process. My dad wasn't there so I felt it was time to become the man of the house. My hormones were just beginning to run wild and my mother and I didn't have the best communication so I fought against being bullied by her orders to do this or that. This of course drove my mother crazy because in her understanding, as long as my father was not living inside our house, she was both the mother and the father and she called the shots.

Rather than racing to become a man, my mother suggested that I become a better man than my father had been. That I thought was impossible because I saw my father as my hero, even in his absence. He was the only adult Black male that I knew. I hadn't known of any uncles or mentors at that time. My dad was a veteran of the Vietnam War. He had to be a tough man. He had to love his children. Something must have happened. Only weak fathers make children and don't stay around to raise them. I was making excuses for him. Everyone seemed to share a similar story about my father, that he was a man nobody messed around with. He was a man with a quick temper who allegedly had no problem using violence against anyone who had an issue with him. My mother told me that my dad used to be a good man but by the time she had already given birth to three of his sons, the streets had a greater calling for him.

Many of my friend's mothers were strung out on crack or could be seen on the streets turning tricks to make ends meet to feed their kids and to pay bills. My mom fortunately never went that route despite how economically hard it was to get ahead during the 1980s. I don't think she had a strategy to get us out of the ghetto or to ensure that we didn't starve, but somehow in 1988 we moved into our newly renovated home on First Street, in the downtown section of Newburgh.

My mother and her friend Mariam had joined in the early 1980s a community-based organization that was aimed at seizing abandoned properties from the City and turning those properties into affordable low-income housing for Newburgh residents. My mother and Mariam were the first two women to move into an historic two-family house with their children. The aim of the organization was to educate and to transform Black renters into homeowners.

Our new home was nothing like the run-down apartment where I spent the first eight years of my life. In fact, our new home won the top award in Orange County that year for successful housing rehabilitation. Our home was equipped with a huge back yard with swings and playground, a sand box, grass, and trees and flowers strategically planted throughout the yard. We even had a fruit and vegetable garden in our backyard that definitely set our house apart from all the other homes in our neighborhood.

I would come to have both good and bad memories of our new home. I would like to think that my actual childhood had its beginning here. Living in our old place on busy Broadway, we were always exposed to everyday crime and hustles of the street people. My mother tried to shelter us from all the crack deals and occasional violence that happened around our building. In our new home, it seemed as if the neighborhood was free of any heavy drug trafficking. But in reality, the corner where my house stood was actually the headquarters of one of Newburgh's biggest drug dealers ever.

In the back room of the popular "Candy Store," as the kids in the area called it, the drug dealer Jerome Stubbs stashed his machine guns and kilos of crack-cocaine. Stubbs was a villain to most folks old enough to remember his husky figure and magnetic personality. Stubbs was alleged to have single-handedly turned the City of Newburgh into a crack haven in the late 1980s. The gangsters in the street however have a different view of Jerome Stubbs. To them he is more of a legend and one of a handful of dealers who ever made fortunes from the drug business. His story is what rappers today rap about in their music. He was the epitome of every drug dealer's dream, known for his massive fleet of expensive cars, diamond encrusted jewelry, and the many East Coast homes he had purchased with drug money. It was his investment in real estate and his aloof presence off the streets that helped him to evade law enforcement for so long. However, everyone knew Jerome Stubbs. He was Newburgh's version of Harlem's Nicky Barnes and the young Rich Porter before Porter's untimely death. Jerome Stubbs became rich from selling crack. He was a ghetto celebrity who flaunted his money among Newburgh's poor, and for this reason many kids in the neighborhood wanted to become the next biggest drug dealer. Jerome sold so much crack that he literally gave hundreds of young men the opportunity to make fast cash. At the same time more drugs in the streets meant more folks addicted to crack and more families disrupted by the plague of crack.

While some respected Jerome, many despised Stubbs for his active role in the perpetuation of drugs in the community. If crack was a tornado ripping through Black homes and destroying lives, then Stubbs was the demon god responsible for this tornado. He was the icon of crack dealers in Newburgh's early crack history. While on one hand he was pumping drugs into the streets and making a fortune, he was also responsible for maintaining minimal peace in the area. Being number one on top of the food chain as the streets' main supplier meant that everyone beneath him had to buy their drugs from him. Therefore Stubbs had very little if any competition and was in a perfect position to make all the money he could before the Feds came for him. He controlled many areas in Newburgh and kept derelict small time nickel and dime drug dealers at bay. Having large areas of Newburgh under his control kept drug related street violence low. Many people agree that drug related homicides began only when the supply of drugs was in too many different hands and the demand for these drugs was at an all-time high. Stubbs eventually became a target for the cops.

CHAPTER 9

MARGARET JOHNS

THE FIRST two years in our new home were perhaps the best years of my childhood. Mother, aware of the potential outside dangers that awaited her children, made sure that our time was occupied with constructive activities. Every day after school before we were allowed to play with our Nintendo or Sega Genesis game system, mother made us finish our homework and read at least a few chapters of a book. Education was pretty big for my mother, having come from the rural South at a time when the importance of education for Blacks came second only to labor. My mother for most of her childhood in the South had to work alongside her siblings on the tobacco plantations to help support her family. Child labor often took away time to get an education. So with her own children, she pushed my brothers and me to do as much reading as possible.

During the summer my brothers and I were either attending summer camp or Aunt Peggy would drive the entire family down South to visit grandma and granddad. They had separated so grandma was living in Ringgold, Virginia, and granddad was living in Milton, North Carolina. The interesting thing was that they were only about ten minutes away from one another so in my mind they were still very much together, just living in two separate homes. If we didn't go down South for the summer, mother would allow us to enroll in the arts and sports programs offered by the Glenn E. Hines Community Center on Liberty Street. The Center was one of the few places in the city that offered kids something constructive to do after school and during the summer.

My mother's friend Margaret lived in Mountainville, NY, a small town removed from urban life just south of Newburgh. She had a special affinity with my mother's kids and the children of mother's friend Mariam. Margaret had a huge heart. She was married to the wealthy H. Peter Stern, former attorney, board member of the International Rescue Committee, vice chairman of the World Monuments Fund and co-founder of the Storm King Art Center. Margaret would frequently surprise us by taking us on long car rides outside the city. She would take us to the rural white communities outside Newburgh to show us the beautiful homes and open spaces of land that were in stark contrast to our urban picture of plight in Newburgh. The most memorable moments of our ventures outside Newburgh were during the Christmas season. Homes were decorated with all sorts of lights and Christmas ornaments that made us feel part of the holiday season. It was a feeling that we were not getting in our own neighborhood. Most families in the hood were extremely poor so they couldn't afford exuberant lights and lawn decorations. Most of us didn't have lawns to begin with and lived in apartments stacked on top of one another so our expressions of Christmas were never unanimous and never filled with that Christmas spirit that the white neighborhoods proudly displayed. When our joyride through the white neighborhoods finally came to an end, Margaret would treat us all to our favorite ice cream which we would delight in until we reached home.

Margaret was generous and always thoughtful when it came to Mariam's and my mother's children. She treated us as her own children and tried to give us what my mother and Mariam could not. I recall the time when Margaret took us to the Metropolitan Museum of Art and later to the Bronx Zoo. That was the first time that any of us children ever stepped inside a museum. We were overwhelmed by centuries of great art and artifacts from all over the world. Going to that museum was like stepping into a time machine and being part of thousands of years of history. Margaret was trying to feed our young imaginations. She instinctively understood how a place like Newburgh could easily suck our young lives into a black hole of nothingness.

Margaret took particular interest in me and we began a special relationship that would sadly come to an end in 2003 when Margaret died from heart failure at 75. But early in our friendship she would take me to the local Barnes & Noble bookstore and allow me to purchase any book of my choosing. Those bookstore trips are what sparked my interest in reading. I was already reading at home but much of what I read was books from school that really didn't stimulate my thinking. Margaret was showing me books that I never knew existed and was encouraging me to read everything my small hands picked up. I ended up becoming an ardent bibliophile way before I reached my teens. Books were my escape from the real life experiences of the ghetto that I could never get far away from. In between every line of a story I read, I could hear a gunshot or a scream or some street quarrel taking place outside my bedroom window. Without such authors as Kafka and George Orwell, who magically transformed my bedroom into another part of the world, I would soon have normalized all of the drama happening outside my home and would have developed a curiosity to become entangled in it somehow.

I met Margaret in July of 1988 when Beatrice Stern, the architect for Newburgh's Neighbors United for Justice in Housing (NUJH) and Margaret's step-daughter, asked Margaret to help my mother and Mariam to plant a garden on the lot next to our home. Margaret was a Landscape Coordinator who helped improve yards in downtown Newburgh for many NUJH families. It was actually the Project Manager of NUJH, Joe Gross, who formally introduced me to Margaret as "The Artist." Everyone involved with NUJH knew about my artistic talent because I was always seen drawing in my sketchbook during the organization's weekly meetings and I was always eager to show off my latest drawings to anyone patient enough to look. I was drawing everyday so it became appropriate for people to start calling me "The Artist."

It didn't take long for Margaret and me to bond. She was a very good artist herself, and since we shared so many interests and she saw that I was full of potential, and her own children, Sarah and Kate, were already adults, Margaret would become my mentor and like a second mother to me for the next two decades. She would be there for me during my most trying times, never turning her back on me. Margaret believed in me. Her compassion and radiant generosity lit up my world as a child. Whenever she came downtown to my mother's house, I knew that day was another opportunity for me to leave the city madness for a much calmer and joyful experience.

In hindsight, yes, it was her white privilege and her wealth that enabled her to move so freely through the ghetto and down to our house to rescue a group of Black children whenever she wanted to. She was in love with us as any mother would be with their children. We weren't her own offspring but our own mothers were extremely poor and destitute with no future for their kids, so Margaret became our surrogate mother, a nourishing presence that we all felt. She was a modern day Renaissance woman – an accomplished painter, a respected research biologist, a writer and educator, a gardener and philanthropist, and that is what made her seem so wonderful in our young minds.

Margaret was born in Boston in 1928 and recognized early for her qualities of genius. She was inquisitive, imaginative, and adventurous. As a little girl she would peruse her father's medical journals, her curiosity piqued by the various physical aspects of disease in childhood.

Margaret would later be recognized as a gifted student. Beginning school at age four, she finished high school by age 16. During WWII she attended George Washington University and later NYU in the 1950s. In 1971, she earned her B.A. in Biology from Hunter College in

New York. By 1979, Margaret received her Ph.D. from the Institute of Animal Behavior at Rutgers University. It was at Rutgers where she would make history by proving her scientific research skills. In her studies of environmental control of ovulation, Margaret discovered the purpose of the mammalian vomeronasal organ (VNO), which was thought by scientists for many years to be non-functioning.

Margaret studied adrenal hormones and their affect on ovulation. Mammalian females are usually separated into two broad categories: spontaneous ovulators and reflex ovulators. Normally, rats and women ovulate spontaneously while cats and rabbits ovulate after copulation. Light levels can affect the ovulating cycles of all mammals, including women. When female rats are kept in constant low levels of light, they cease to ovulate. When exposed subsequently to the appropriate light stimulus, the female rat will ovulate.

Margaret discovered that copulation was not necessary to induce ovulation in her rats. Instead, brief exposure to the urine of male rats was sufficient to trigger "reflex ovulation" in low-light-induced non-ovulating rats. But Margaret was not sure if it was a sense of smell that caused the ovulation. In time, she would learn that if the female rats were separated from the male urine by a slight distance, they did not ovulate. Utilizing a fellow student's technique of cauterizing the VNO, she closed off the VNO of her rats, so that when she brought the female rats into direct contact with the male urine, they did not ovulate. Margaret had made her discovery. If the VNO is closed off, there is no ovulation. Those with VNO intact ovulated. Margaret's discovery caused uproar in the field of olfactory studies. At least one scientist quit the field after 40 years of research rather than have to repeat all his published experiments.

Margaret once explained to me that even she had her moments of despair and setbacks. Being a woman in the scientific field was not easy, she would say. Men in her field tried almost everything to thwart her from reaching her research goals, even attempting to steal her discoveries.

In 1980, Plenum Publishing printed Margaret's major article that she had read at a symposium. The article was titled, "The Role of the Vomeronasal System in Mammalian Reproduction Physiology." Then in April of 1996, the Wall Street Journal published a story on California researcher David L. Berliner, a former professor of anatomy and founder of the Pherin Corporation, a small company developing products with odorless chemicals called pheromones, which could treat a long list of ailments from PMS to panic disorders.

In the article, the reporter wrote: "Researchers had assumed for years that in mammals, pheromones are detected by the sense of smell. But in 1978, Margaret A. Johns, a doctoral candidate at the Rutgers University Institute of Animal Behavior, reported that in the lower mammals a tiny pit in the nose was the pheromone-sensing organ. Physiologists and anatomists had known of the pit, called the vomeronasal organ in animals for more than 150 years, but had been baffled by its function."

Then Berliner himself wrote a letter to Margaret saying that, "There can be only one discoverer. That is you. Without Margaret Johns, there would be no field." Margaret was a scientific genius and would be an inspiration to me for much of my early life.

CHAPTER 10

THE DRUG JUNGLE

SHORTLY AFTER we moved to our new home on First Street, the drug supplier Jerome Stubbs was arrested and convicted of enough weapon and drug charges to keep him behind prison bars for at least 20 years.

One would think that it would be commonsense for the police or local government officials to protect the neighborhood from the emergence of any opportunist drug dealers, aware of the fact that Jerome was now out of the picture. But there was no neighborhood protection; no intervention by city officials; no drug treatment programs set up to address the addiction of the drug users in our community. As soon as Jerome Stubbs was removed from Newburgh several gangs spontaneously sprouted on the blocks surrounding my home, all attempting to sell crack where Jerome once did.

The night scene on Lander Street soon became reminiscent of the Broadway nightlife that my mother tried so hard to protect us from. First and Lander Streets (see map of the neighborhood) became ground for turf wars, deliberate and indiscriminate shoot-outs between rival gangs. Crack heads and crack dealers were once again all part of the street canvass. Our new neighborhood was a drug trafficking zone and now that my brothers and I were old enough to venture outside alone, we were now exposed to it. And it always felt like there was no escaping the madness outside our home that went on from sun up to sun down.

Crack dominated our streets during the 1980s and 1990s. That was the drug of choice then and young Black men, often isolated from the workforce, made an occupation of hustling this narcotic. It was easy money and easily accessible. It was easily packaged and easily distributed just as well. Selling crack was a first job for many young Black boys before ever thinking about a real 9 to 5. There were quite a few major movies that debuted around this time that glorified selling crack and amped up young people to get into drug distribution, especially if they could become as large as the movie characters Nino Brown and Scarface, and get rick quickly. Crack kept young dealers posted on any street corner that had a flow of addicts. And with more dealers came more killings. I had picked up early that Black life was cheap and disposable. The old-timers in my neighborhood called my city "The Graveyard." My city had earned that name because on practically every street in the city someone had been shot or stabbed to death. My city even competed with other much larger cities nationally to be labeled the city with the highest homicide rates. In fact, for a long time, my city did hold the record as the per capita murder capital of New York State. Already by my first year in junior high I had too many friends who lost their lives in the streets, or I had heard about teenagers who were shot dead. Violence was pervasive and seemed to be what Newburgh was all about.

Teenage girls plotted fights after school in the park not too far from the school. Friends of mine like Peanut and DeShawn would bring guns to school and would brag and show off these steel toys in between classes. My friend Maurice was just 16 years old when he was shot in the neck and nearly paralyzed. So much violence was happening that despite how tragic things were, everything felt normal. There was never a time-out moment for us to reflect on what was taking place. Shit happened every day and that was our mental conditioning.

People just considered death to be part of the daily routine of being young and back in the ghetto of Newburgh. I think we all accepted the possibility of dying young.

On the block where I lived, Da Original Dark Side Gang or DODS managed the blocks from Chamber to Johnson and all of Lander and First Street. They called this area El Barrio. So much crack had been sold on that block that Lander Street would be dubbed Crack Alley. The name Dark Side probably came from the fact that at night, El Barrio became pitch black due to the street lights being busted from getting shot out. Walking through the Dark Side at the wrong hours could cost you your life. If you weren't from that side of town, you were bound to end up a victim. Two blocks from the Dark Side was South Miller Street or South Millions, named for its constant flow of dealers and heavy traffic of white drug buyers coming into Newburgh from neighboring towns. Because South Miller ran off Broadway and directly into First Street, it acted as both easy access for drug buyers and as a fomenter of brawls among rival drug dealing cliques.

Du Bois Street also had heavy drug trafficking and cliques of its own. Jamaican marijuana and crack dealers controlled the blocks of City Terrace and Van Ness, Lutheran, and the upper half of First Street. Jamaican dealers gained control of those blocks once a young dealer known as Pat Patterson and his goons were arrested and broken up by police for drug dealing and illegal weapons possession. South Street was known as the Ave. It was north of Broadway and was controlled by the Ave Boys. The south side of Newburgh was known as the Heights and had its share of everyday dealers and gangsters. I wasn't from that side of town and didn't have many friends that lived over there so I didn't travel to the Heights very often.

These ten or so blocks were the heart of the inner-city of Newburgh. They are what made the city a jungle where only the brave-hearted could survive the ills which plagued Newburgh. No one was really safe in the jungle of Newburgh.

How you survived was determined by the role and the price that you were willing to play and pay.

Either you played as the prey or the predator. Trust me, I feel horrible having to use such primal and predatory terms to describe my city. And I would never blame the victim. But Newburgh was a concrete jungle and living there meant keeping your eyes open at all times. Get caught and poof!. . .the streets will gladly claim your life. Gangs, cliques, drugs and hustlers ran the jungle and it was either join the wild animals or be eaten by them.

CHAPTER 11

A DEATH IN THE FAMILY

I WAS maybe ten years old when mother came to my bedroom, downstairs in the basement of our home, and told me the somber news that my Uncle Thomas had died. "Died!" I said beneath my breath. I didn't really understand what she meant by death. I remembered people dying on TV but appearing later in other shows, sometimes coming back to life in the same television program. My mother tried her best to explain what death really meant to me, seeing the puzzled look on my young face. All I remember hearing was my mother say something about God and that people are called home and that I will never see Uncle Thomas again. Religion was never a big deal in my house, so much of what mother tried to explain went in one ear and out the other. I was stuck at the part about never seeing my uncle again and couldn't fathom that.

Death had never occurred before in my family. I thought that we all lived forever. What was the purpose of life ending? No one had ever mentioned to me that one day we all would have to suffer death and be buried under the earth and seen no more. Mother never told me, and none of my elementary school teachers either, that life is short and that in the blink of an eye, we are gone. Hearing of Uncle Thomas' death made me sick to my stomach. I remember feeling paralyzed. I would lie down in my bed and try to make sense of it all. I thought hard and deep, racing through the thoughts of my adolescent mind. We are born just to die! We are born just to die? I would ask myself this question and then look up to the sky, where I had been taught that God resided and ask God the same question I had asked myself. But I got no answers. I would scream out loud, louder and louder to outer space but I would hear nothing, no voice responding back giving me the answers that I needed to hear. I would just cry and plead to God. And cry some more. I locked myself in my bedroom and cried until I could cry no more. There weren't any more tears in my dried out eyes. I had come to the dreaded conclusion that we were born just to die. As improbable as this was for me to digest, I thought about my family having to die one day. I thought about myself dying, right then, in that very moment, at any moment. My life tomorrow was not promised. I could easily fade away and be gone forever. So why was I here? Who put me here? What was my purpose in this life? My puerile mind searched for answers but found nothing.

Just as I could not hear God's voice, I could not muster enough faith to believe in a God. I was too young to have known anything about being an atheist, but I was damn sure close to being one because God was a fantasy to me. I became a skeptic, cursing God every chance I got. At times when my two brothers and I were forced to attend church, I would sit in the back pews with the other children making mockery of the Deacon or Pastor as they preached about Redemption, Heaven and Hellfire. All the poor Black folks sitting in this hot church, praying to another man, a white man at that, nailed helplessly to a cross, made no sense to me. Why couldn't Black folk pray to a God who resembled them and why was it that Black people in church were always suffering and shouting in distress.

The years would fly by after Uncle Thomas' death and I noticed that my questions concerning death, and my thoughts about it did not waiver. I had spooked myself. I would become haunted by the thought of death for the rest of my childhood.

Dying was always on my mind and to some extent, still is. My fear of dying had in some strange way affected how I lived my life. I felt like I was always on pins and needles. Living but not living fully, in fear that death was always near. It was almost like an infatuation with dying had manifested itself, and thinking constantly about it was liberating and at the same time traumatizing. I would sometimes walk past the local funeral parlor on Chambers Street, just to view the corpse resting motionless in the coffin. I did not know who the dead were or how they died. None of that mattered. What mattered to me was that I wanted to face my fear of death and the sad reality that I one day would be resting motionless in a coffin.

CHAPTER 12

SUMMER'S FIRST MURDER

I WAS was 12 when I witnessed a murder up close for the first time. It was summertime in the city and mid-afternoon. Everyone was outside doing their own thing. Adults and children were moving about and some were settled on corners and in front of bodegas and other small businesses. It was a typical day so nothing out of the ordinary stood out. I was on my way to pick up dinner at the Caribbean Restaurant on lower Broadway, just two blocks from my home. I hadn't been out long when the murder occurred. At first all I heard was the commotion. Then people began running. I was no more than 20 feet away in the street when I heard the gun go off. I heard guns go off at a distance, but this was very close, so to my virgin ears it sounded like the sky split in half by the striking of thunder. The blast made my ears ring and the vibration continued down to my knees. I was shaken up but it was all over in a few seconds. Everything around me was still on pause. The scene was surreal as it unfolded with people still ducking and dodging.

Right in front of me his Black body crashed into the sidewalk pavement. He was already stiff and lifeless in mid-air. His fall sounded like a sack of bricks smacking the concrete. The shot left his head and brains partially removed; his face was covered in his own red plasma. It was a shocking sight and something that will be stuck in my memory forever. The dead man was an older Black guy; completely unknown to me. He could have been in his late thirties or early forties. But now he was dead. I later learned that the facts of age and name mean very little out in the streets when another person feels disrespected. Disrespect usually ended a person's life; all life at any time could be treated as cheap and disposable.

The two teenage boys who did the shooting ran swiftly past me, trying to escape before the police made it to the crime scene. One of the teens held a shotgun in his hands. I stood there motionless, trying not to be present. A speeding car skidded around me, beeping its horn consecutively, reminding me that I was standing in the road. I quickly got myself together and ran home. Part of me would feel guilty for not staying there with that man. He died there on the street alone. I never found out what became of those two teens or the identity of the man they killed. A few years later, homicides in the city would become commonplace and it became easy to become immune to seeing or hearing about people dying. A good friend of mine would often say that Newburgh was a city full of orphans due to the number of kids who lost their parents to gun violence. One day I would come across a passage by the poet Maya Angelou and be moved by it. It explicitly spoke of what I had witnessed and what I was feeling at the time. Her passage read:

> "In those bloody days and fruitful nights when an urban warrior can find no face more despicable than his own, no ammunition more deadly than self-hate and no target more deserving of his true aim than his brother, we must wonder how we came so late and lonely to this place."

CHAPTER 13

GROWING UP COOL AND AFRAID

JUNIOR HIGH School was the place to be. It was a new freedom, far from that slave camp of elementary school where my friends and I were always supervised and scolded for every little thing we did wrong. It was a world of new faces and opportunities and seemed a whole lot safer than the gritty and grimy streets. Junior High was my escape from all the adolescent madness that I was going through at home. My plan, like most teens entering junior high for the first time, was to be free from constant teacher surveillance and to have fun, meet new friends and score with the girls. And there were a lot of girls to explore, more than the same faces of the girls I had grown to hate during six long years of seeing them every day in elementary school.

I had no idea that junior high was as big as it was with so many students I had never met before, kids from different neighborhoods and sections of Newburgh and the town of Newburgh. Junior High was a new place to explore. I hadn't realized how sheltered my mother had kept me until I began interacting with other teens in school. Most teens my age had already been deeply exposed to the dark life of the hood and knew all the ins and outs of street culture. The hallways of my school mimicked a street corner before the period bell rang to notify us that classes were in session. Kids were smoking weed in the bathrooms, chasing all the pretty girls, and emulating the older guys back on the neighborhood block. It was all about running with a crew and looking as tough as you can. Looking tough was a language in itself in the hood and was just as important as knowing how to navigate your way through the streets. It was part of the ghetto persona to act hard. That façade kept people from fronting on you, if they sensed that you weren't weak. School was no different. Street rules often crossed over into the school domain and no one wanted to be singled out and bullied. Just as playing hard would keep you alive a little longer in the streets, it would also keep crews in school from making you the subject of their unwarranted beat downs.

I wasn't born with the face of a brute. I had far from the face of a young Mike Tyson, chiseled with anger and fearlessness, ready to eat a person's heart out. I was clearly the opposite. I sported a high flat-top fade hairdo like the 1990s Hip Hop group Kid-N-Play. I had soft but bold facial features: long dark eyelashes, bushy eyebrows, full lips, and golden brown skin. Girls admired me and dudes in school envied me. They called me a pretty boy. I wasn't much of a talker in this new environment and I came off as shy. But my shyness was considered cute by the girls. I just knew that I was a good looking kid and despite not having much game, I figured my looks were enough to pull new girlfriends. But pulling girls couldn't account for the things I lacked that would make all the difference in school when it came to being cool for the fellas.

The fact that I grew up knowing more about books than I knew about video games or cared about sports was just another character flaw that made me different. I was a nerd at heart but always wanted to blend in with the others. Being smart in high school was uncool and made me feel uncomfortable. Plus my peers didn't respect that kind of difference. My smarts made them feel dumb so I usually left the show of brains to the white students. I was still into art at this time and found myself sketching in my notepad during boring lectures given by my teachers.

In Junior High there were circles of crews. Most days I could get away with hanging out with other artists and the cool nerdy kids who actually enjoyed reading. But these kids were the minority. Everyone else seemed to be into fashion, smoking weed before during, and after school, and into the drama that was happening downtown. A lot of my friends were already hip to the lingo of the street— the street possessed its own lingua franca understood by the thugs and dealers. It was more than the use of curse words and slick talk that our parents would scold us for using. Street lingo was a coded language that only those who were down could use and participate in. It was the language of a secret society of goons and gangsters who wanted to defy the cops and all of white society. This is before Ebonics (a Black dialect) was accepted by the mainstream and before Gangster Rap became part of popular culture.

White people were secretly called "Crackas" behind their backs and we called other Blacks "Niggas" because it sounded slick and we pretended to sound like our parents and uncles who talked this talk. Nigga for us was not a convoluted nostalgic term. It had nothing to do with reawakening the racial hatred that whites had towards Blacks in the past. *Nigga* meant that one was a bona fide legit person. Sometimes white boys who were cool with us became our Niggas as well. But white boys weren't permitted to use that word under any circumstances. Only Black people reserved the power to toss that word around even though whites had invented it. Those white boys who were foolish enough to say Nigga ran the risk of getting punched in the face.

Some vocabulary was still exclusive to the hood and even still, only the cool street-initiated knew when and how to use certain terms. Street vocabulary was correlated with street psychology, easily mirrored, and followed certain behavior. Talking the talk sometimes wasn't enough. Most times you had to walk the walk or be called out for bluffing. The street terminology that was floating around in the hallways and staircases of school was new to my ears and I was desperately trying to learn it all. At the same time I was trying to figure how to mesh my own soft features and artsy image with the socially accepted rugged look of the gangster.

Leaving school and heading back downtown was always a dreadful walk. I knew that I had to walk past most of the blocks where the gangs and crews hung out. I always carried the fear of walking on the wrong block at the wrong time and getting jumped, robbed, or shot. Gangs took their turfs seriously. It was their home – a place they owned and congregated and had to protect. Any outsiders were subjected not just to the scrutiny of long cold stares from the beginning of their walk to the end, but sometimes also getting beat up for disrespecting a gang's turf. Mastering ghetto slang and having that tough image was important in moments when you were cornered and confronted by a gang. Sometimes you could talk your way out of a beat down by claiming connections to a certain set or stressing your neutrality. There is both strength and fear in numbers so sometimes claiming association with a larger gang could save you in a smaller gang's territory. Claiming false association could also get you killed. So claiming a gang was as dangerous as claiming to be neutral. Your biggest hope was that the gang would recognize that you were the younger brother or nephew or cousin of someone from the same gang. That would save you from getting hurt. I didn't always have that luck.

Because my house was in the middle of conflict territory, I had no other choice but to walk through the Ave, down Dubois, and down First Street past South Miller and Johnson – all active gang hoods. You were fortunate if you had a big family in Newburgh and a few known live wires as brothers or uncles to help fight your battles. I didn't have any older brothers or uncles around and my dad had disappeared a few years earlier so I was forced to fend for myself.

The streets were a place where you had to fight. Fathers taught their sons how to fight. Mothers made sons get up off the ground and defend themselves. When friends fought, their friends had to jump in. If I found myself about to get into a fight and was lucky enough to be close to my house, my mother would run outside and make sure that it was either a fair fight or no fight at all. That's how it was in the hood, but when the gangs seized neighborhoods, parents had no answer when it came to gangs and gang violence. Most gangs were already terrorizing the neighborhood and left clear messages that they weren't to be messed with. A lot of my friends were walking on eggshells in our own backyard. I was feeling like my back was against the wall and if I became a target, I better be able to defend myself.

The attacks and robberies continued. It became more than bullying. It was older teens looking for an easy target just to get their frustration out or to steal a few bucks from a younger defenseless teen. After a while the punches, kicks, and bruises would no longer affect me. I was dead inside and what kept me alive was not my heart beat but rage. Part of me was crushed and another part of me wanted revenge. I wanted to pay them back for jumping me and robbing me and making my life hell. I wanted them to pay for disrespecting my mother every time she rushed outside to save me from being pummeled by my attackers.

Growing up in the hood made it easy to begin fearing your own kind. The cops were one thing to fear, but it was more hatred for the cops than fear. The cops harassed us only when it was convenient for them or when they suspected that Black boys were up to no good, which was probably always the case. Most times the cops had no idea what was going on unless someone had snitched. To a large extent, what was happening behind the curtain of the hood was sheltered from white eyes. It was largely only in public performance – entertainment and sports – that we shared with a white audience the complexities of Black life. For the media we put on this act of being white America's greatest fear as they watched us through a fish bowl. They knew that our wretchedness was contained. And no matter how bad things became or how tragic the latest crime happened to be, the media still fed us back our own plight. Black dealers sold drugs to Black crack heads who lived in the same building as the dealers and Black stick up kids robbed other Blacks who lived in the same neighborhood as they did. And amidst all of that there were good Black folk who were subject to all of this. Good Black people have the same fears as good white people. Nobody asked to live next door to pedophiles and dealers. But being Black and poor, we don't have the privilege of choosing who our neighbors are, or just moving away.

The media would play into and instigate a fear of Black men, even by other Black men. It was almost as if a conspiracy was active between the media and street culture to put young Black boys into a kind of fear-death ritual. When my mother watched the nightly news, I would recall the melodramatic musical instrumental come on and the news caster chime in by informing us that it was such and such time, did parents know where their children were? That would frighten the hell out of me. Then a story about a Black rapist or killer on the loose made it impossible for my two younger brothers and me to go to sleep. In my young mind, I would swear that the horrible things I saw on television, combined with the everyday gossip of corner loiterers, was all part of a scheme to keep my mind locked on a Black predator lurking around the corner, watching my every move.

It was as though every Black man was a threat to my life and was out to kidnap or murder me. At least this is what the media wanted me to believe. The few roles that Black men played on television were largely that of criminals, liars and buffoons. Even most Black rappers took on the names of and emulated dangerous men and criminals. Black youth in my neighborhood easily believed in these images because they were shown on television and were hardly ever countered by more positive Black images in the community. We sometimes internalized those images and tried to live up to the name and legacy of our role models, even if it was against our best interests.

Black fear of other Blacks was coupled by messages from my mom or sisters that little Black boys aren't supposed to cry. We are supposed to hold those tears back and suppress our pain, shelter all that hurt inside us. Become emotionless and heartless if we had to. But shed no tears. Tears were for girls. Tears were for sissies. No tears, and never run, not even away from bullies. Black boys don't get bullied. We don't get terrorized. Black boys are supposed to be the ones who victimize people and terrorize communities. Black boys are supposed to destroy lives and to menace other Black people and if possible, white folks as well. This is the thinking of many, and many Black parents teach their sons this. Maybe, just maybe, they are right. Maybe that notion is true, in light of the society that Black boys must grow up in. Maybe we have to be thugs and overly aggressive and tougher than others. If we did not hide our emotions, the world would see how vulnerable we truly are. Or worse, the world might even get to see our humanity. What would happen then?

CHAPTER 14

MY ONE BLACK MALE TEACHER

MR. MORGAN was my ninth-grade science teacher and the only public-school teacher who actually gave a damn about me. His warm welcomes and his knack for greeting his students with a "Hello sir or young lady. Time for science!" was sometimes enough to get at least half of the class interested in learning about atoms and animal anatomy. Most of us respected Mr. Morgan and knew not to act out in his class – in fear that he would give us a piece of his mind and tell us off.

Unlike many of the white teachers in school, Mr. Morgan did not fear us. He didn't come to work with predetermined doomsday attitudes about us that the other teachers held. Even when some of the more seasoned class clowns would find ways to disrupt the class, Mr. Morgan would remain calm and would use a disruption as a catalyst for a biology lesson. Most of his lessons would begin with a dissertation on the death of a species due to its lack of moral compass and intelligence.

Mr. Morgan had no problem calling students out and demanding an explanation as to why they chose to spend 50 minutes of their life as an unpaid comedian rather than a disciplined student, when education or the lack of it would definitively define their future.

Mr. Morgan was one of three Black teachers I had in my primary grade education and the first and only Black male teacher I've ever had. By the street standards of that time, Mr. Morgan was the farthest thing from being cool. He was already old and certainly did not measure up to the Black men back in my neighborhood. In a weird way I suppose I looked up to Mr. Morgan because he was different and he didn't have any hardness that made him unapproachable. His presence I assumed meant that he cared. If he could come to work every day and attempt to teach us, he had to care about us when many of us didn't care about ourselves. I mean, we had pride. Most of us were full of pride. We just didn't believe in our futures.

Some of us were actually illiterate and to hide that fact acted out. Or we had serious issues going on at home and school was the only opportunity for us to express ourselves for the few hours we had there. Our teachers didn't understand that we were really just trying to buy time. We all sensed that something awful was approaching us so having fun was the only way we knew how to deal with that kind of pressure. And I think every student imagined school grounds as a safe haven. It was the one sacred space where Black and brown youth didn't die. Looking back, I think that Mr. Morgan as a Black male and an educator understood the larger idea that Black and brown youth were failing because of their lack of participation in their own education. His daily frustration proved this. But Mr. Morgan did not know how some of his Black male students were really close to trauma. His science lessons weren't equipped to heal or protect us from the grim reality of our lives.

I believe that Mr. Morgan saw unusual talent in me. I recall like yesterday times when I would not do the right thing and he would bring me back on track by calling on me to answer a question in front of the class. "*Mr. Jones, can you please name for the class the known parts of an atom? And after that, please explain to the class Einstein's thoughts on Dark Energy.*" Mr. Morgan called on me when I was being a knucklehead, but also because he knew that I knew the answers. He sensed early that beyond my attempts to play cool and at times to be the class clown, I was really a bright student who was selling himself short.

By the time I was eight years old I already had an interest in nature and was fond of biology even though the inner-city certainly was devoid of the types of species and wild life that we would study in class. But that didn't limit my thirst for something more. In my young curiosity I would play with frogs found in my backyard and by night my brothers and I would use glass jars to capture Lampyrida (fire flies) because we were so fascinated by their glowing florescent abdomens. That was the thing about nature; science was always around me even in my real urban world, if I looked closely enough. Way before I was able to fathom the criminality and injustice of man, I was in love with science and how things worked. The stars in the night sky amazed me. Thunder was an awesome sound. Worms, snails, snakes, and most creepy crawling things excited me. I wanted to know why they were here, just as much as I wanted to know why the sun burned fire and what kept the Earth revolving on its axis around the sun.

Mr. Morgan's class honestly spoke to me and fulfilled me in many ways. It wasn't always theoretical. Sometimes it was hands on where we would perform dissections of frogs and other amphibians. Examining the anatomy of these small creatures actually took my attention away from my fear of the real dangers that existed in my neighborhood. Science made me feel like the world was mine, mine to explore and master. It served the same purpose that art had served in the earlier years of my life. I felt free and not under an adult microscope with science and art. They made me feel part of the world and the universe, and not unwanted and despised as most everything else in my life made me feel at that time.

CHAPTER 15

DANVILLE, VIRGINIA

EVERY SUMMER since I was six years old, my mother would send me down to Danville, Virginia, to stay with my grandfather and Uncle Thomas, until his death. I appreciated spending my summers with granddad and Uncle Thomas, but I hated country life. I was a city boy, used to concrete and bright lights on top of tall buildings and loud music. Where granddad lived, there was nothing but tobacco farms and acres of unused land all around. Danville was as "country" as country could get.

There were no other children around my age, just granddad, Uncle Thomas and me. Occasionally one of my granddad's nephews would come by but they were all much older and had very little time for me. Granddad's house was just short of resembling what a slave shack would look like. It was made of thin concrete and chicken wire, the same chicken wire used for housing chickens away from coyotes and foxes. Granddad was far from wealthy but he was self-employed. He was a small farmer and before that a sharecropper for a white man who owned a colonial-style mansion and several acres on the same road as my granddad. Back then farming was mostly what Blacks knew and my granddad took pride in agriculture. When he was a little younger, he was a prize fighter like the American Negro boxer Joe Johnson but not as popular as Joe. When his career ended as a fighter, he went into the business of farming, selling his produce to the local markets of Danville. His father was a tobacco farmer and alive during the era of slavery. Granddad was born in 1910, three years before the Abolitionist Harriet Tubman died and four years before World War I. Every day he would have me out in the field either watering the plants or picking tomatoes or peas or corn. Vegetable picking always came with a story from granddad that made working in the dirt much more fun. Granddad always had a story to tell about African ancestors who once walked this land and of the Dakota Tribe of Sioux Indians that his parents and grandparents also had a biological connection with. During slavery, some slaves and free men would escape and integrate into Native American communities to avoid oppression by whites.

Besides the shabby look of granddad's house, it felt as if it was nestled in the middle of nowhere. His house was completely surrounded by uncut weeds and bushes, standing at least five feet tall. There was a wooded area on the right side of the house with a trail that led to a fresh water stream. Every morning granddad would have uncle Thomas and me walk down to the stream with a wagon full of empty milk jugs to fill up with water. Drinking fresh water from a stream was something that I couldn't do back home in New York. Up North, houses had bathrooms that were part of the interior of the house. Granddad's bathroom was behind the house and wasn't much of a bathroom at all. It was an out-house often occupied by the smell of feces, flies, and if unlucky, a black water moccasin that uncle Thomas would have to shoot dead because I would scream for my dear life whenever I saw one slithering around the out-house. I hated everything about that out-house and could never get used to it.

Each day after my work was done on the farm, granddad would give me a half dollar coin. He knew that I was amazed at the size of a half dollar and the fact that two half dollars made a whole dollar. When you are young simple things like coins amaze you and having a collection of half-dollar coins made me feel rich.

One evening granddad sent me to the store alone to pick up a few groceries. Although it was less than 100 yards away, I had never walked to the store alone before. What seemed like a casual walk to the store would become an adventure. A white family, the Hudsons, owned the store. The Hudson's store was far from the bodegas found on almost every other corner back in Newburgh. When I got to the store, Mr. Hudson and his family were all standing around talking. I could have sworn that all eyes were on me as I walked about the store looking for the items my granddad asked for. Feeling nervous was an understatement. This was the South and I understood the South to have different rules from up north. So I was walking on pins and needles.

When I found what I was looking for and purchased it, I walked out of the store, hoping to quickly make it back home safely. All I wanted to do was to get back to granddad's house before those white men inside Hudson's store got any ideas. I was paranoid. Ten minutes of walking was ten minutes too long. I was lost. The weeds and bushes surrounding granddad's house made it impossible for me to locate it and there were no other visible landmarks that could help me.

The overwhelming weeds were staring down at me like monsters. I tried to retrace my steps, walking alongside the towering weeds on the right side of the road. Granddad's house was nowhere to be found.

My only option at that moment was to go back to Hudson's store and tell someone that I was lost. I began walking toward the store fearful of what danger I might be placing myself in. When I reached the store, I walked inside and approached the counter where the cashier stood. I told the cashier, an older white man, that I couldn't find my granddad's house, that I was lost. He asked me if I was Daniel Allen's grandson. Without hesitation I said yes, surprised that he knew my grandfather's name. Mr. Hudson said that he would drive me home. I was relieved and at the same time apprehensive. I remembered the stories that granddad and my older cousins shared with me about the racism they had faced in their day, of how when they were growing up, on any given day you could expect to see a Black boy or man hanging from a tree by a noose. I remember granddad making me listen to Billy Holiday's chilling song, "Strange Fruit" – a rather morbid and symbolic song she wrote about the lynching of Black men and boys in the South. Granddad would have me examine the extreme hatred of racism found in young Emmett Till's mangled body, an image that would stay with me forever. Danville wasn't Mississippi or Alabama, but it was still the South and enough to have me on edge about this white man driving me home.

Mr. Hudson was not a racist and certainly not a man interested in lynching me. He was actually a long-time friend of my family and known as an honest man. He drove me to my granddad's house safely. Whether there was any dialogue between the two of us in his truck, I cannot remember. I just wanted to get home safely and quickly. I don't think I ever went to that store again or left granddad's house alone.

Granddad's friend Willie would come by the house once or twice a week in his rust covered 1950 Chevrolet pickup truck. Willie's truck had enough space for only two passengers, so I had to sit in the back of the truck. I didn't mind however. The wind was freedom as we rode down all the back roads in Danville. I enjoyed the sun and having a clear view of all the surrounding scenery. We would drive through the countryside of Danville where granddad and Willie would point out to me all of the large plots of land that were once reserved as slave plantations. Today they stand as barely managed tobacco fields or the territory of cows and horses. Before our day came to an end, we would stop at the local Piggly Wiggly, a major supermarket chain in the South, to purchase enough food and supplies to carry us through next week until Willie would come for us the following week to go shopping again.

CHAPTER 16

CRIPS AND BLOODS

I WAS about 13 years old when my friend Chaz and I decided to make a pact while in his backyard. We were tired of being pushed around by the older guys in our neighborhood. We had been friends since we were seven or eight years old. I was maybe a year younger than Chaz, but we both had seen enough on the streets of Newburgh to understand that if we weren't tough out there or had our own crew, then we were as good as dead. In Chaz's backyard, we both agreed that we would have each other's back no matter what. We agreed to become brothers. We became blood brothers.

During the summer of 1993, we met an older teen named Andre. Andre was maybe 17 or 18 years old at the time and claimed to have come from Los Angeles. We really didn't know where he had come from. But we respected Andre because he was older and had heart. He was the type who wouldn't back down from a fight and who was always caught up in some kind of drama. He stood about six feet tall and had a fierce look in his eyes that said he was not one to mess with. Chaz and I idolized him.

Andre was not your average teen from the streets. He was street smart and militant-minded. As I remember him, he had street maturity about him, a street edge that made every word that came from his mouth worth listening to. During the summer of 1993 he would teach us his street philosophy, the politics of California ghettoes, and the reasons why Black youth turn to gangs or "families" as he called them. He spoke of Cali as if it was the blueprint for the rest of American urban ghettoes. He had enough scars and gang tattoos on his body to back up his every word. Andre was the first Blood we had ever met. He was a member of the Five-Nine Brims.

Beyond our everyday missions to find schemes to get money and to raise hell in the hood, Andre would hold pow-wows with us in Chaz's backyard. We were learning about the Bloods and the Crips. At that time Newburgh didn't have any allegiance to these nation-wide gangs and was dealing only with homegrown cliques born on neighborhood blocks. Much of what Andre was kicking to us was over our heads. We had never been to California and we heard about the Bloods and Crips only from the movie "Colors." The only thing that was making sense was that we were starting our own gang in 1993. We recruited about six other friends from the neighborhood and started calling ourselves PTH or the People That's Hard Gang and we imitated the West Coast Bloods by adopting red as our gang color. The fact of the matter was, we knew nothing about gang banging and had no reason to at that time. We weren't slinging drugs and claimed no block as our own. We were just a gang of kids fascinated with Andre's talk of gang ideology and we wanted to be down with something greater than the homegrown cliques that Newburgh had at the time. Later on, the uncle of one of our crew members came home from the federal penitentiary in Missouri and changed our gang name to GMF, which stood for God's Moorish Family.

Andre's lessons didn't always fall on deaf ears. We were listening. We just weren't connecting anything he said to what was happening in our young lives. Andre was trying to teach us how the Bloods and the Crips were the last desperate attempt by the Black Power Movement to empower, organize, and mobilize America's urban Black ghettoes. We just took it as if we were supposed to be like some badass super heroes doing something righteous. The only thing we were really doing was hanging out and committing occasional juvenile delinquent acts like breaking windows and stealing bikes.

When I got older I got hipped to the Cali scene and really began to digest gang culture. Before gangs had really taken root in the urban Black psyche, the Black Power Movement was gang culture's predecessor. In Oakland, California, in 1966 Huey P. Newton and Bobby Seale created the Black Panther Party for Self-Defense. The Black Panthers would combine Black Nationalist ideology that leaders like Malcolm X were preaching with Marxist-Leninist doctrine from the Communist Party. The Panthers hoped to fashion the party into a revolutionary vanguard dedicated to overthrowing capitalist society and ending police brutality. The Panthers believed that Black people were not just disenfranchised American citizens but victims of colonization. The ghetto was a colonized space, according to Huey.

The Black Panthers, dressed in black leather jackets, berets, and Afros, alarmed white Americans when they took up arms for self-defense and patrolled their own neighborhoods to monitor the police. In Oakland and Chicago, the Panthers arranged free breakfast and health care programs, worked to install racial pride in Black children, lectured and wrote about Black history, and launched some of the earliest drug education programs. These ideas and programs made the Panthers popular to Black people but made them even more of a threat to the white establishment.

A combination of these efforts by the Panthers caused FBI director J. Edgar Hoover to infiltrate, harass, falsely imprison, murder, and to ultimately destabilize the Black Panther Party. In August of 1967, Hoover distributed an explanatory memorandum that detailed the FBI's counterintelligence program directed toward Black Nationalist groups. The purpose of this new counterintelligence campaign was to expose, disrupt, misdirect, discredit, or otherwise neutralize the activities of Black Nationalist, hate-type organizations and their leadership, spokesmen, membership, and supporters, and to counter their practice of violence and civil disorder.

Undercover agents infiltrated the Panthers and provoked violence and criminal acts. Police informants and agent provocateurs committed most of these criminal acts but the blame was placed on the Panthers. In their effort to destroy the party, law enforcement officials killed an estimated 28 Panthers and imprisoned 750 others. In perhaps the most egregious incident, police in Chicago killed Panthers Fred Hampton and Mark Clark while they were asleep in a predawn raid on the Illinois Black Panther Headquarters on December 4, 1969.

In the Panthers last attempt to survive the brutal campaign of the government, they attempted to organize young brothers and sisters in street gangs. Andre was telling us how all that rage and hopelessness went into the brewing ingredients that gave rise to the Bloods and Crips. Black gangs were really supposed to avenge the defeat of their parents, the Black Power Movement. However, the inability of the Black Power Movement to remobilize itself within the next generation of urban Black youth caused street gangs like the Bloods and the Crips to become the total antithesis of the Black Power struggle.

The leadership of the Black radical intelligentsia in America was crushed and left no serious alternatives or programs for urban youth. So in turn, the Bloods and Crips were left with political or revolutionary names (BLOODS - Brotherly Love Overrides Oppression and Destruction; and the CRIPS - Clandestine Revolutionary Internationalist Party or Continuous Revolution in Progress) but with no true political aim or direction.

The generation of youth who found themselves belonging to the Bloods, Crips, and other street gangs, are the children of little hope and enormous disbelief in the so called American Dream. These youth are the historical children of men and women who were slain by the U.S. Government for their political beliefs and willingness to stand up against a morally bankrupt and racist society. They are the bastard offspring of America's long and enduring culture of violence, and the failed attempts of Blacks to be legitimately interwoven into mainstream America. The Bloods and the Crips are in a sense a symbol of urban Black youth's rejection and abandonment by both the dominant white culture and the Black middle class.

So for the past 40 or so years, urban youth in their desire for attention and love have been on a campaign of "gang-banging" for social recognition. Gang-banging is killing and waging war on rival gangs in communities all across the nation. This phrase would make sense to me during my incarceration. Countless Black and brown youth in prison were banging on one another for no real reason other than recognition and acceptance and the fact that gang bangers shared the same position of powerlessness as other gang bangers.

I came to realize that it is an act of cowardice and denial to be standing on the periphery of urban genocide and to condemn the phenomena of urban Blacks killing other urban Blacks like suicidal piranhas, and to do nothing about that genocide. Vilification and criminalization are easy. That is America's easy way of disposing of what it does not wish to deal with non-punitively. The real challenge is understanding and peeling back the layered psyche of rage, and generations of unanswered frustrations and neglect, that have left urban youth voiceless and visionless. The truth is that many young people turn to gangs or street tribes because they feel rejected by their own families and by the larger society. Those responsible for American youth have created machinery that grinds up their young and fails to ensure an environment that provides those most unfortunate a meaningful path to self-discovery, social-identification, and self-respect.

Gangs become their new family. In gang culture, children feel they are someone of value. The gang has their back and purports to ride to the death for their family members. Instead of feeling alienated and disrespected, they are protected and even honored by their home boys or home girls. They discover purpose, a reason to live and quite often a mission worth dying for. They are allowed to be themselves without having to conform to the destructive, paternalistic and racist norms of society. They are not sanctioned or censured by their peers, and they acknowledge a "love" from their gang that they otherwise never received from biological relatives or social institutions.

By the end of summer in 1993, Andre was in all kinds of trouble with the law and with other teens in the neighborhood. He could no longer be in Newburgh lest he end up in juvenile lockup. So his family sent him upstate to Albany to live with another family. He would come down to Newburgh every so often and hang out with the crew. He was like our OG (an "original gangster" is an older mentor who survived the dangerous streets of Newburgh). He gave us street wisdom to survive and he had helped to form our crew. I, Chaz, Travis, June, and a few others were the PTH (People That's Hard) Gang and we bonded to have each other's back and to remain brothers until death.

CHAPTER 17

SOMETHING WORTH DYING FOR

TO LIVE and die for a name was our only aim. A street reputation is everything to a Black kid who has not been taught his true self-worth. A street reputation is to ghetto youth what a college degree is to mainstream society. To live and die for a name is like chasing after the wind. Ghetto youth are baptized in sin, so used to losing we all want to win. Winning could never be counted in money and riches. We live our lives for fame. We just want love; we just want a name. Gangster, Thug, Menace, Keeping it Real! At the end of the day these names mean nothing at all. Those who chase after them in the streets always seem to end up dead, in prison, or undoubtedly bound to fall.

At 13 I thought that "keeping it real" was something that I was supposed to find in the streets – hanging with the homeboys, smoking marijuana, g-riding through the hood with your middle finger raised high at the cops and anyone else who was opposed to our keeping it real.

At 13 I believed that "keeping it real" was always putting yourself on the front line for your homeys. I thought "keeping it real" was breaking curfews, sneaking out my bedroom window, looking for unnecessary trouble, raising hell in school, getting chased by the police, and living life on your own terms. At 13, what did I actually know? I knew that I was watching most kids in my generation try to prove their manhood in the streets. It was always about going that extra mile, pushing yourself beyond the limit, proving that you were more insane than the next kid.

Someone once defined insanity as repeating the same thing over and over and expecting a different result. I've seen the type of insanity that grips and often strangles the ghetto. It is a type of insanity that is born out of ignorance of the law and of life. It grows from a deep feeling of social and economic deprivation. We felt deprived of life and of the joys we expected to come with it. We tried to become part of something that we hardly understood. We always wanted something more. We grew up watching white success and whites triumph and believed that we deserved the same. In our chase for life we ended up overdosed on death. Death came full speed at us. We ran towards it with open arms.

At 13 I was a scrawny kid searching for an identity in a world that was still unknown to me. My world was intimidating and full of terror. I was tired of being terrorized in my own neighborhood and tired of terror altogether. I was tired of running from constant threats so I stopped running. I started to fight back. But at times it was no use. I was always outnumbered or physically dominated by the older kids in my neighborhood. And my crew wasn't always there when I needed them.

I was tired of being the underdog. I was tired of being the victim. Even at 13 I refused the word victim. It felt so powerless. It felt like I was giving up my right to defend myself. I had to find a way to affirm my manhood or what I thought was manhood. I wanted to be a part of the crowd and to prove that I was down. Trying to be down, however, would get me into serious trouble with the cops in Newburgh.

I had a series of bad dealings with the cops. My crew and I were committing petty juvenile acts like vandalism by spray painting graffiti on property and skipping school to play video games. We weren't doing anything really serious but serious enough to get the cops to know that a gang of youth were on the loose. We were always getting accosted by the truancy officers or harassed by cops for loitering in front of local businesses. My last encounter with the police occurred when I was in possession of a stolen bike that I had borrowed from one of my friends. I was riding the bike through the Heights when an unmarked police car pulled up beside me. At first I was taken aback when the man in the car began to yell at me about where I had gotten the bike. Then it dawned on me that he was a cop and I was in possession of stolen property. I tried telling the officer that I had borrowed the bike from a friend but once he started to get out of his car, I took off running. I had no intention of getting nabbed for a bike that I was only borrowing for a simple joy ride.

I couldn't outrun a cop car that was bent on catching me. I was apprehended. The angered cop threw me into the back of his car. All I heard was racial epithet after epithet and questions about where I got the bike. We finally reached the juvenile delinquency building, adjacent to the police department. I ended up in the cop's office since I was too young to be processed in the main building. There the interrogation began again. But this time the cop was holding a shotgun at my head, loading it with large red colored shells and his finger on the trigger. I was his "Nigger-Boy" for the day, according to him. It was just him and me in that room and no one was there to save me. I thought I was going to die. He certainly put enough fear in me that I would think twice about riding a stolen bike again. But it wasn't enough fear to make me snitch on my friend. I ended up telling the cop that I acted alone in stealing the bike from a backyard. Loyalty was everything in those days. Ironically, a decade and a half later an officer would kill my friend I had borrowed the bike from when the policeman placed him in a chokehold during an arrest.

I never did get criminally charged for having the bike. I think the cop understood that he was just as wrong for putting a shotgun to the head of a teenager so he finally let me walk out of his office, completely terrorized.

CHAPTER 18

BLACK AND LATINO TENSION

RACIAL TENSION has been an integral part of Newburgh life since as far back as I can remember. The tension is mostly the clandestine kind that only a few are able to recognize and name. Conflicts between the Black and the Latino communities have gone on for well over 20 years. But poor Blacks unified with poor Latinos have always taken issue with the City of Newburgh police over police brutality against racial minorities. Newburgh has had its fair share of racial riots proving that racial injustice is deeply rooted in the culture of the city. Most Black folks living in Newburgh have a story or two or three or four about problems that they or someone they knew have faced with racial conflict. If you talk to the Latino community in Newburgh, there are those who feel threatened by the Black community, and some have accounts of being victimized by a Black person.

For the most part, this tension existed due to both groups viewing each other from a competitive economic point of view. Both communities were faced with extreme poverty. Both communities were conscious of the fact that they were a community of "have nots." Realizing that real power and money belonged to the white community, both groups wanted their piece of limited local power and resources.

What greatly fueled the tension between them were misconceptions and stereotypes each group had about the other group. The poor Black community witnessed large influxes of Latino families migrating to the inner city of Newburgh, believing that jobs denied or not available to Blacks would somehow be offered to the Latino community at below minimum wage, thus, forcing Blacks into deeper poverty – a poverty ripe for demoralization and a rise in crimes of desperation. The Latino community on the other side viewed Black poverty as a social threat to Latino community development and assumed that Blacks were lazy and shiftless and refused to work if jobs weren't paying well.

So both groups had their guards up high, playing defense. Any time the Latino community opened up small businesses in the neighborhood, they were viewed as emulating white shop keepers who were seen as concerned only with Black dollars. The Latino community rightfully protective of their resources and businesses, failed to bridge gaps between themselves and Blacks. Instead they treated Blacks as if they were criminals and people who could not be trusted in Latino stores.

Throughout the 1990s, there were ethnic wars on the streets of Newburgh. Of course, calling conflict between Blacks and Latinos an ethnic war is a stretch for the white American imagination. Minority racial groups born and living in America for the most part have never exercised a cultural or political autonomy that gave them a status far removed from their historic designation as slaves, subjects, and criminals. Unlawful behavior by these two minority groups was always criminalized, but never understood for what it really was – ethnic clashes over a small piece of the American pie.

Blacks caught in Latino sections of Newburgh would be confronted and beat down by a mob of chain and steel pipe wielding Mexicans. And if a Latino person was found walking through Black neighborhoods, they would get robbed and assaulted unless they were fast on their feet and could escape.

Mickey was only 14 when he was caught walking on the wrong side of town. A gang of Mexicans chased Mickey through several blocks, until he was finally out of breath and surrounded in an empty parking lot by a gang calling themselves the BBK or the Benkard Barrio Kings. Strapped with weapons and the tribal rage of catching a Black kid on their territory, they tried to kill Mickey. They cracked his skull, broke one of his ribs, and left him covered in his own blood. Luckily Mickey survived that incident. Anyone surviving or walking away from an attack like that was considered a soldier in the hood. Mickey had earned a few stripes for going through that but now he had to prove himself through a get back. Retaliation was obligatory in the hood. Returning the bloodshed was expected, and any Latino found in the Black neighborhood was supposed to get it. There was no innocence, only ethnic identity. It didn't matter if innocent blood was spilled. Everyone was always subject to becoming victimized, or at least that was the attitude on both sides. Your skin color determined what side you were on. We were all enemies and both sides saw it that way.

In the mid-1990s to guard their neighborhood against Blacks, Latino youth were forming cadres of the National Latin King Gang on Newburgh streets. Also, in the Mexican section of Newburgh, some Mexican youth were calling themselves MS 13 (Mara Salvatrucha), a gang originating in California. However the most dominant gang in the Latino community proved to be the Benkard Barrio Kings. The BBK established themselves as one of the most ruthless gangs in Newburgh's history, corrupting and terrorizing the streets with murders of rival gang members and the spread of cocaine and heroin.

Between the Jamaican gangs uptown, the handful of African-American cliques downtown, and the Latin gangs in the Heights section, it was constant war and strife in the streets of Newburgh.

This war would reach its climax during a party on Broadway in the summer of 1995. It was a local house party and like most house parties, no invitations were given so anyone was likely to show up. At some point during the party a feud developed between some Latin

Kings and a Black clique from Chamber Street. A scuffle broke out and a Black youth we knew as Bam was stabbed to death. Bam was well known and loved by many people in the hood so someone would have to pay for his death. Retaliation would follow with several home invasions of Latin King members. Sooner or later those responsible for Bam's murder would be found and punished in retaliation.

About a month or two after his death, the Latin King members involved in Bam's death were found in one of their hideout houses. They were retaliated against. One was shot dead and the other shot in the head but survived. The survivor testified against the shooters and three Black youth were convicted and sentenced to prison. That was the end of one battle, but the street war was far from over.

CHAPTER 19

ROBBED AT GUN POINT

EVENTS WOULD occur in the 14th year of my life that would deeply affect my self-perception and how I understood the world around me. These events would place tremendous strain on me. I would come to learn that Black children are treated differently from white children in many instances. A white child and a Black child may experience similar traumatic injuries, but will be treated with two entirely different approaches. Depending on the severity of the traumatic experience, the white child in almost every case will receive some form of therapy as a necessary means of overcoming the effects of the traumatic experience. The Black child on the other hand, after experiencing a traumatic event will not undergo any form of therapy or treatment and will be forced to live with the trauma with no help. That is having to live with the emotional and psychological strain and to suppress the memory of the trauma. Suppression of the traumatic memory comes as a natural process for the Black child to ensure survival. But the emotional experience of the trauma we live with every day and we learn to become numb whenever faced with anything remotely close to the initial trauma.

When Black children are forced to suppress their emotional frustrations and fears stemming from their experiences, this suppression leads to a de-sensitized personality, so that events and experiences that would be traumatic to any other child or adult become normalized in the reaction and attitude of the Black child. In other words, in order for Black children to survive the extremely negative and threatening conditions of the ghetto, they must become detached from or desensitized to their own environment.

November of 1994, before Thanksgiving, was the first time that I was robbed at gunpoint. Getting robbed or "stuck up" was something that could happen to anyone in the streets. I would always hear about this one or that one getting robbed by the local stickup kids. You really had to have eyes in the back of your head and couldn't trust anyone. Sometimes you couldn't even trust your own friends. All it really took was getting caught in the streets, in the wrong place at the wrong time. It became a general rule always to be strapped with a gun just in case someone trying to run your pockets confronted you. I was 13 and didn't have access to a gun even if I wanted one. Not having a gun became pivotal to my life. Not having one, I felt my life taking a downward spiral toward a dark place.

During the entire year of 1994, I had been saving money that I had earned from my summer youth job at the recreational park and the little side hustles I did around the neighborhood. I was also saving my monthly allowance, which was never more than a few dollars. I was grateful however because most of my friends at that time weren't receiving any money at all from their parents. I had been saving all year to purchase a popular NFL Starter jacket and matching hat. Every kid in my neighborhood either had one or talked about getting one. You weren't cool if you didn't have a Starter jacket. It was a must that I get a Miami Dolphins jacket with the matching hat, and if lucky I would find a pair of sneakers to complement my whole outfit. In the streets we called that "keeping your cipher complete," a line from Nas' *Illmatic* Album.

I recall the day when I was robbed at gunpoint. It was about two weeks before Thanksgiving Day. It was a clear but rather chilling morning and I had just left my house around 10 or 11 o'clock, hoping to be one of the first customers at Brian's Sport Shop, a sports and hip-hop clothing store owned by Asians on the uptown end of Broadway. Getting robbed was the furthest thing on my mind that morning. I was not even three blocks away from my house when two older youths accosted me with one brandishing a gun. They threw me into a hallway and began to force the nose of the gun into my neck, pressing so hard that the gun felt like a sword they were using to sever my head from my neck. While one kid had me pinned against the wall, the other was searching through my pockets. My initial reaction was to fight them off and get the hell out of that hallway. I think that in my initial shock, with my adrenaline rushing, I even thought about suffering a gun wound in my back instead of letting these stick up boys get away with my hard-earned money. But my shock quickly dissipated, turning into a combination of emotions. Fear, rage, and anger ran through my mind simultaneously. A part of me was infuriated for allowing myself to get caught out there— everyone had to expect the worst when they walked through the hood and it was the responsibility of every individual to move about as inconspicuously as possible. The less you are seen, the better your chances of survival out there. The other part of me just couldn't believe that I was getting robbed. I was in disbelief. It just didn't seem real. I was defenseless in a hallway with two older kids with a gun, bent on taking whatever I had on me.

As I was being searched, I stared deep into the two robbers' eyes. I was numb of course, forced not to move. The only activity that showed that I was still alive was the movement of my eyes burning into theirs. I wondered just how these two Black boys could even think of robbing me. I was a younger version of them, Black like them. I could have been their younger brother since I was at least five or six years younger. But color didn't evoke brotherhood or protection from violence. Because we were all Black, it made it easier to harm and steal from one another. Their focus was my money. My age obviously didn't matter.

A look of frustration came over the face of the one who was searching through my pockets. I began to calm down, knowing that as long as they searched through my pockets they wouldn't find a dime. Mother had taught me that while walking through these streets the best place to hide your money is in your sock. Their adrenaline was racing just as fast as mine. They were trying to get the job done as quickly as possible without getting caught or before things escalated or backfired. I was praying to God that they didn't search my socks, but in their desperation for money they were willing to search every possible hiding place on my body.

When they found the money, all $300 and some change, they took off leaving me in the hallway. I stood in that hallway for a long minute, trying to regroup myself. The hallway was lit only by the sunlight penetrating through the glass panels in the wooden door. I left that hallway and began to walk toward my house. My anger and disbelief was so intense that I didn't feel the chilling air beating upon my flesh.

When I reached home I didn't bother telling my mother what had happened. I was embarrassed to tell her that the $300 that I had worked hard for was just taken from me. Never mind the fact that this time the robbers put a gun to my face and that I could have been killed. I couldn't tell my mother what happened, not this time. Besides, what could she have done but made my situation far worse. I'm the one who had to deal with these streets every day. The demons in the streets were demons that I would have to face, not my mother or my sisters. So I wanted to keep what had happened to me from them. I would find my own way to deal with it, in my own time.

I locked myself inside my bedroom, pacing my room thinking about the robbery. Many thoughts flashed through my mind. I fantasized that if my father was around or if I had older brothers and uncles around, things like this would not be happening to me. Or if I were rolling with a gang, $300 would not have been such a big deal because I would probably be selling drugs and could easily make that money back. My gang and I could easily roll on the kids that had robbed me to get my money back and teach them a lesson that they deserved. I so wished that I had walked a different way earlier that morning. Broadway was not a good idea with all the wolves lurking. I tried to rationalize that I should just take this as a loss and forget about it. But I wasn't going to forget about it. That was a whole year's worth of hard work, including raking leaves in the fall and shoveling snow during the winter. There was no way that I could forget about my money. But what was I supposed to do?

Mother had noticed that I came into the house that morning with no new NFL Starter jacket in my hand. So she did what any mother would have done, she came downstairs to my room to find out what was going on with me. She questioned me about the jacket and the money and after trying to make up an alternative story to tell her with no success, I was forced to tell her what had happened to me that morning.

Mother was both disappointed and angered. She insisted that something must be done. Since she didn't believe in using violence to solve problems, she said that we must get the police involved. I didn't want to go that route because getting the cops involved is never a good thing while still living in the hood. But my mother wasn't having it. No one was going to rob her son with a gun and get away with it.

"Right" things in the hood almost always seem to turn out wrong. Mother tried to convince me that getting the cops to do what they get paid to do was not only the right thing to do but also the only realistic option. "They put a gun to your head, boy. They could have killed you. You have no choice but to tell the police what happened to you," mother shouted. She said that taking matters into my own hands would only lead to greater problems for me. Besides I was only 14, so what was I supposed to do against older teens with a gun? So we got the cops involved. I had no idea that my decision would ultimately open up a Pandora's Box, unleashing a world of unforeseen troubles and problems for me.

After explaining what had happened to me over the phone, the police advised my mother to bring me down to the police department to see if I recognized the two men in a photo lineup. A part of me was already influenced by the philosophy of the streets. I knew enough that I didn't want to be labeled a snitch and have to deal with any retaliation. Snitching was a street taboo. Another part of me didn't want to let my mother down or to let those robbers get away with taking my money and using a gun to do so. Mother didn't care about some stupid street rule. As far as she was concerned, her 14-year-old son should never have been robbed, and the robbers should be punished.

At the police department the officer that I spoke with on the telephone greeted us. He brought me to his office and showed me a large photo album book. All I remember seeing was hundreds upon hundreds of Black faces, stacked on top of one another. It reminded me of those illustrations of the inside of slave ships where human cargo was piled together like sardines. There were young Black men and old Black men; Black men with corn rows, dread locks, bald heads and Afros; Black men with scars on their face, birthmarks and tattoos; Black men with light skin, brown skin, and dark skin. They were my brothers. These Black men are all my brothers. Criminals or not, I saw kinfolk. I did not see my enemies or specifically the two teens who had robbed me. I really did not want to be in the office of a cop. I wanted to run out of that police department with the pictures of all of my brothers in hand, never looking back. In the face of every Black man staring at me from their photos, I felt their pain. They all spoke to me, revealing their own anger and bitterness, but their songs were all the same. We are at war with the System but losing. We are at war with each other but losing. We are killing each other, hurting each other, sabotaging one another. I wanted to run, not only out of the police department but also away from the war. In that police photo lineup album, I had seen my whole race. It was symbolic of my whole race. And they were all screaming at me, demanding a redemption that I could not provide them. I knew that I could not carry their pain. Not now and not ever. I knew that I did not want ever again to allow myself to be anyone's victim. I should have grabbed that photo lineup and run as fast as I could. I started to, with the intent of symbolically freeing all of the Black faces trapped forever in that police album, but then I noticed the faces of the two young men who had robbed me at gun point. The fire of rage rushed throughout my body and if my eyes were fire I would have burned a hole straight through their eyes as I stared intently at the two thieves. It would have satisfied my mother if I told the police and probably would have satisfied me too, but I just could not force myself to give them up to the police.

Apparently I was not the only person to have been robbed by these two young men. They were eventually arrested for a string of armed robberies and pleaded guilty to those charges. And although I had nothing to do with their arrest, Pandora's Box still opened and for several months after that I would be followed home and harassed by friends of the two men. I had to constantly watch my back. Sometimes I was imprisoned in my own home, unable to go to school on a regular basis or just hang outside my house without the threat of having to fight.

I became paranoid, forever having to watch my back, not trusting anyone, and even at times had to walk in the middle of the road because I did not know if someone was lurking behind a parked car or building waiting to shoot me. If I did not recognize a suspicious face walking towards me, I would change course immediately. I just didn't know what to expect and was trying to avoid getting killed. I was so unhappy with the world around me. I thought about suicide but that was not ever going to happen.

About seven months after the robbery, one of the convicted kids had gotten out of jail and with three other kids with him, we had crossed paths. I was with my friend Jason, a hip white kid who lived next to the high school, and my girlfriend Mecca. We were heading downtown to my house. With no words exchanged, one kid threw a punch and the others followed suit and I found myself in the middle of swinging fists ducking and swinging back with all of my strength.

I was trying to hold my own for a while but they were getting the best of me since I was outnumbered. I wasn't expecting much from Jason since I was already outnumbered but that didn't stop him from jumping in and helping me. He had pulled one of the kids off me and was swinging wildly at the kid's head. The next thing I know, Jason was holding the side of his face. The same kid who had held the gun to my neck during the robbery had sliced his face with a knife. My girlfriend jumped in front of me acting as a bulwark and with Jason bleeding, they ran off. We got away from what could have turned out worse than a few bruises and scrapes and a small cut on Jason's face. We were shaken up, no doubt. My girlfriend was crying but Jason and I both knew that we had survived. Things were probably going to get ugly, but for now we were okay and that was what mattered. This time anyway.

CHAPTER 20

THE POWER OF A GUN

SINCE MY childhood I have always dreamed of becoming a great scientist, moved and awed by the splendor of the possibilities that existed far beyond the reality of the ghetto around me. With Margaret by my side as my mentor, the mysteries of the universe and the complexities of nature captivated me in ways that always left me with more questions than answers. This kind of exploration as a child greatly contributed to an objective quality in my thinking that fostered my ability to observe everything around me realistically. Paying careful and curious attention to movement and sound and the very evolution of life that was taking place all around me became essential to my thinking, even after my dreams of being a scientist faded and just surviving out there in the streets became primary. The older I became and the more involved I was in the streets, I recognized how fast things were changing. There was a strong, menacing attitude in the air. By the summer of 1995, this negative aura literally swept over Newburgh and seized people.

In that year, the rate of gun violence and gang assaults in Newburgh exploded. The air was more dense than usual and the streets were in flames from the intensity of violence that was happening out there. All my friends and the older guys on the block were more alert, and people just seemed to be moving differently, more carefully. I would come outside and feel a silence that blanketed my block. We all were waiting as if for a bomb planted by a foreign terrorist to detonate. But there weren't any foreign terrorists. Instead, the only acts of terror and violence were coming from rival blocks and gangs waging war and starting drama that almost always ended with someone dead.

I vividly recall someone either getting shot, murdered, robbed, or another gang rolled on some block in a drive-by. Whether you were involved or just a spectator, everyone was affected by the violence. Especially in Newburgh, because the city was so small that everyone either went to school together or our mothers were friends or we were related in some way or another. The tension was so thick that you could feel it. Certain territory was forbidden to even walk through. There were No Walk Zones where, if you weren't permitted to walk through them, you were risking your life.

This increased violence in the streets would sooner or later come close to home. First, one of my friends from elementary school, Maurice, was shot in the neck and almost paralyzed in a drive-by shooting. Second, I knew that most kids in my neighborhood were either already packing a gun or had access to one. But it was a kid who I went to school with named 'Fat Cat' who actually showed me what a gun looks and feels like. I had never held a gun in my hands before.

I'm not sure that first feeling could ever be described. It was a feeling of power that I know young Black kids from the ghetto do not experience without a gun. I felt bigger than life; strong and invincible. I felt like I was every superhero I had ever watched on television, now alive and in flesh, materialized by the weapon I held in my hands. The unique feeling of control that overcame me seemed supernatural. I suddenly understood the power of holding a gun in my hands.

I knew immediately that this was the very instrument that would prevent me from dying in the streets. I really wasn't concerned about, nor did I truly understand, the possible consequences of using a gun. I certainly didn't believe that I would ever be forced to use one. I knew that a bullet had penetrated the living room wall of my mother's best friend's house. The bullet crashed through her window after she had called the police about a drug dealer selling drugs in front of her house. Mrs. Cook and my mother were friends for well over 50 years. They became friends shortly after my mother arrived in Newburgh from North Carolina in 1967. Mrs. Cook, like my own mother, was a child of the Civil Rights Movement or at least of the climate that it had created within most urban communities. Black Mothers took pride in where they lived and took it upon themselves to keep their properties clean and as safe as possible against drug dealers and hoodlums.

Mrs. Cook was a community-conscious woman who cared about her neighborhood. Her keeping our block clean and helping to maintain a colorful assortment of flowers in the backyard garden demonstrated the pride she had in our neighborhood. Mrs. Cook was also one of the best Southern-style chefs in the area. Everyone loved her cooking and would request her fried chicken or macaroni and cheese and collards every weekend. But despite how well she cooked, some street people on the corner didn't appreciate her presence. They considered her "the nosey lady in the window" who would call the cops when she noticed illegal activities. Mrs. Cook wanted the best for her community even if others didn't.

After the Neighbors United for Justice in Housing community improvement program was established in 1988, the women of the organization decided to police their own community in a de facto Neighborhood Watch Program. Any loitering, drug sales, shoot-outs or fights, were enough for the mothers in the community to call the cops. They weren't exactly working in partnership with the police. The mothers were fully aware of the systematic racism that existed in Newburgh that often made cops come off as routinely apathetic to Black ghetto crime. But at the same time the mothers understood that they themselves were no match for drug dealers and gangsters. So pushing the police to do their work was the mothers' way of taking back their community. It eventually became clear to everyone at NUJH that the police were interested only in attacking surface level crime while ignoring the roots of crime in Newburgh, which meant going after the big drug suppliers and not just the small nickel and dime dealers. The women of NUJH would receive another lesson about the streets when calling the cops too many times moved a drug dealer to attempt to teach Mrs. Cook a lesson. That's when a bullet came crashing through her front window. Luckily no one was injured.

CHAPTER 21

LEARNING TO USE PRISON TIME

I HAVE never tried to escape the facts of my life. I understand clearly that I am totally responsible for the evolution of my life and how the decisions that I made will determine my future. As a teenager unconscious of my own power over myself, I had no idea that I was writing my own destiny by the choices and decisions that I was making. That was a personal power that I didn't think about and no one had ever made me aware of. And I believe that not knowing of this responsibility made me powerless over an environment that I was at war with and that was destroying my potential for positive growth and development. What does not destroy you makes you a little more resilient but it also leaves behind stains in the mind that cannot be easily wiped clean. These stains are a residue from bad experiences that damage your memory, remain in your subconscious and forever keep you paralyzed, not realizing that you can escape the ghetto. My greatest challenge was to realize that my negative encounters in the streets were not my fate and did not have to define my future. Just because I witnessed more than my young eyes should ever see, and my confrontations in the streets had burned bad impressions into my mind, I did not have to be a slave to those negative emotions and experiences. I could choose to be brutally honest with myself and seek a mental and emotional freedom. I could heal myself and clear away the pain that I had accumulated in my mind.

Being removed from the streets at the age of 15 was a scary experience. I left one world that was confusing and always dangerous to me and was thrown into prison without warning or instruction. All of the fears that I had about dangers in my streets were now collected right in front of me. I now lived among the criminals I feared at home and there was no escaping them. The only thing that separated me from everyone else was a steel cage with only a flat sheet of metal bed affixed to concrete walls, a dirty sink and toilet. That safe separation was only momentary however. Soon the prison cell door would open and I would have to face the reality of prison life.

Spending time away from society isn't always a bad thing. Some good can come out of a bad situation. One thing that is always available for the condemned is time alone. Time is the one possession that a prisoner is allowed to have. The judge can remove you from society and take away your freedom. But the judge could never take away the space between you and the person you can potentially become. Time is a blessing for those who recognize its value. There is a power of healing in time spent alone. I can't say that I was fully aware of the potential uses of time at the onset of my prison sentence. I was still a minor who thought as a minor and conceived time as minors do. I believed that the years would fly by and I would eventually be home again, back in school and hanging out with friends. I thought that everything would be behind me and I could start my life all over again without ever having to recall the past. That of course would not be the case. The years dragged by slowly and holidays and birthdays of family members were missed. The year of my graduation from High School came and went. Each year I was getting older and feeling less free as new and younger convicts were entering the prison system. I was a witness to convicts who had prison identification numbers before I was born, growing old and dying in prison. I would share conversation, games of chess, and sometimes food with prisoners who were in their 20th and 30th year behind prison walls. Prisoners would reach their maximum sentence and be released, only to return to prison, sometimes only months later. That revolving door was all too real and was pushing me to lose hope about my own release from prison and what awaited me whenever my time for freedom came.

I refused to lose hope in prison and refused to become just another condemned convict destined for the monotony of concrete, steel, bizarre prison food, and years spent trapped going in and out of that revolving prison door. Many of the prisoners were already hopeless and had given up a long time ago. They had come from nothing and had nothing to go home to. Some had caused so much damage and destruction on the outside that remaining in prison was safer for them than to return home and end up facing the consequences of their crimes or in other words, street justice. That kind of prisoner found it easier to make a home out of prison and possessed no intention of ever returning to the streets. They disgusted me. They were complacent and well-adjusted to everything about prison. They were so conditioned to prison that there was a compatibility between them and the prison guards. Those prisoners whole routine was to maintain the continuity of prison, even if conditions were oppressive and not conducive to a prisoner making it out alive or ever reaching true rehabilitation. I learned to stay far away from them and from the prison guards whose inhumanity stemmed from their realizing that their job security rested on me staying in prison for the rest of my natural life.

Time would not be my enemy. I couldn't just walk out of prison, but I didn't have to live as a hopeless prisoner either, and didn't have to subscribe to the prison mentality that never leaves you once prisoners allow themselves to become institutionalized. I wanted to know what about me or what about the streets had pushed me toward the use of violence. I also understood it to be imperative that I begin to assess everything about who I was that put me inside a prison world designed for people unfit for freedom. My thought patterns, emotions, beliefs and ideas, everything had to be scrutinized, challenged, and discarded if found to be the cause of my prison sentence. I figured that there had to be something intrinsic in my culture that was sending me and countless other Black youth and men to prisons for crimes mostly committed against our own Black community. I was thirsty for clear answers and would use my prison time seeking them out.

CHAPTER 22

TAKING RESPONSIBILITY FOR MYSELF

TAKING RESPONSIBILITY and ownership of my destiny was a huge part of my prison transformation. I had to own up to a lot of things that I didn't want to admit to and even had to question the idea that we are the product of our environment. I couldn't be the product of my environment and at the same time declare that I was the master of my own destiny. I had to accept responsibility for almost everything in my life if I ever wanted to become the person that I knew I could be. I had to rid myself of the old me that made incarceration even a possibility in my life. I had to accept the reality that had I not owned an illegal gun, I wouldn't be incarcerated and another young man's blood would not be on my hands.

At the age of 15 I found myself in a precarious situation. I felt like it was me against the world and I was at odds with everything around me. My own Black body became a vessel of frustration in which I found myself in constant strife with other Black bodies, and at the center of white rage whenever I was confronted by cops. I remember on several occasions I would lock myself in the bathroom. Standing in front of the mirror I would loathe the image that I saw. I didn't hate myself. At least I didn't think I did. I had always thought of myself as being proud of my heritage or the little that I knew about African history. But for some reason, I found myself hating the body I was in. It was my nose, my lips, and my brown skin, that made other Black boys and the white police attempt to beat the color off my body.

Feeling that I was caught in the devastation happening in my community, I was trying not to fall victim to a cyclic path of destruction. Youth my age were getting destroyed regularly. Some of them were getting locked up and others were getting murdered. It felt like we were disappearing. And I felt powerless. I felt trapped in a city falling apart. My exposure to violence and the senseless killings around me made me paranoid and feeling like I would soon die. The strange thing was that most of us weren't trying to be negative. But it seemed that no matter how hard we tried to be positive we were subjected to becoming victims in the streets of our own hometown. At 14 a gun was pointed at my head in a robbery. And on at least three other occasions after that I was standing in front of the barrel of a gun facing death or injury. I had to live through the sad reality of this madness.

I know that I am responsible for the choices that I had made in my life, and that I am responsible for the kind of friends I chose to be part of my life. Those associations I realize today played a major part in what I was exposed to and how I decided to live my early life. Negativity breeds negativity, and when I found myself surrounded by negative people, it was unlikely that I would muster the courage to respond in any manner except what seemed acceptable. That is by no means justification for what I did and how I chose to live in the streets. I am the first to admit that some of my gang's behavior was barbarian; we were destroying our communities and ourselves. Taking responsibility for our lawlessness and absolute disregard for our communities and the people in them is the only way that we can open up the possibility for change. I couldn't blame the white man or the white system for what we were actually damaging with our own hands. I know that a lot of things weren't right in our community that the local government was responsible for. But in the end that was no justification for us to be running wild like teenage animals.

I needed to understand this in order to overcome the blame game. I did not want to blame myself for all of the crime and savagery of the streets. But blaming others for how we lived was irresponsible and produced inactivity in ourselves. It was just as important for me to put into context that some of the wrong inflicted on me was done by individuals who themselves were hurting from wrongs done to them. Hurt people hurt others, so it was the reciprocation of all that pain that I believe accounts for much of the crime in my community. Understanding victimization within the Black community, and how we were prone to lash out at each other because of internal pain, helped me to abandon the idea that there was something innately evil about Black skin that made it a target.

A lot of us had internalized that idea and were driven by it. I'm not sure how and when it happened, or who specifically encouraged us to do so, but we had internalized the degrading passions and motivations of our white oppressors and had adopted their worst behavior toward our own kind. We became our own worst enemies. It baffled me that no one had ever brought this understanding to my attention before my incarceration. The profound ignorance that reigned over our streets was unchallenged. Black people weren't having intelligent conversations that could diagnose the behavior of Black criminals. Schools, churches, and other institutions within the Black community ignored the forces that cultivated the worst in Black youth. It was as if they had denied the history of oppression in this country and had avoided the only plausible explanation that there had to be an internalization of the worst values that were once thrust upon Black people by white slave holders and white communities.

CHAPTER 23

DOUBLE CONSCIOUSNESS

IT WASN'T until my 18th birthday, while in a youth detention center, that I developed a serious curiosity about urban Black psychology. It was my dear friend Margaret who on my 18th birthday sent me a copy of W.E.B. Dubois' *The Souls of Black Folk.* Dubois' work was perhaps the most eye opening book for me at that time. His work, writing and accomplishments were inspiring. I had never heard of him before and never knew of any Black man who thought the way he did.

Dubois had written that, "After the Egyptian and Indian, the Greek and the Roman, the Teuton and the Mongolian, the Negro is a sort of seventh son, born with a veil, and gifted with second-sight in this American world – a world which yields him no true self-consciousness, but lets him see himself only through the revelation of the other world. It is a peculiar sensation, this double-consciousness, this sense of always looking at one's self through the eyes of others, of measuring one's soul by the tape of a world that looks in amused contempt and pity. One ever feels his two-ness – an American, a Negro; two souls, two thoughts, two unrecognized strivings; two warring ideals in one dark body, whose dogged strength alone keeps it from being torn asunder...."

Dubois' analysis of what he called "double-consciousness" read like poetry to my ears. His words spoke directly to what I was feeling. Dubois' words were the key that unlocked the heavy negative self-perception that had fettered me in my youth. The acceptance of my own inner conflict, I believed, would reveal everything about me and help me understand how I and other Black youth thought and felt about our relationship to other Black youth and to the world around us.

Dubois' writings set me in search of the deeper meaning of the self-hatred of Black youth. I began to read anything that I could get my hands on concerning young Black males. Luckily a few staff members at the Harlem Valley Youth Detention Center would smuggle in books for me to read. Certain books were prohibited by the detention center, and staff was not allowed to bring in anything for the residents, but since I was seriously interested in learning and self-study, they made an exception to the rule.

I was reading at that time from Haki Madhubuti's *Black Men Obsolete, Single, Dangerous?* to Jawanza Kunjufu's *Countering The Conspiracy To Destroy Black Boys* to everything written by Dr. Na'im Akbar. The depth of my understanding was growing fast and I was developing new language and context. Being young and Black was no longer a blemish on the American canvass that brought about negativity and only trouble. I was seeing for the first time how multi-layered we were and how history revealed that American society, in all of its racism and hegemonic displays of white supremacy, had shaped the rules of engagement for young Black males.

A few staff members who knew I wasn't a knuckle-headed resident who would rat them out, were sneaking me books one after the other. I never could understand why certain books were considered contraband. During routine searches of our rooms, some staff were adamant about searching my room to find materials they could deem contraband. Anything that they could say related to Five Percent doctrine, pro-Black philosophy, or gang-related literature, was sure to get me thrown in solitary confinement. We never knew when these random searches would take place. So to prevent them from confiscating my books and throwing me in solitary, I would read and take notes simultaneously and once finished with a book I would pass it on to the next resident.

One day I got my hands on an Amos N. Wilson book and I was blown away. In his writing titled *Black on Black Violence*, Wilson underlines some critical points that I took seriously. He explained the terrible act of Black on Black violence as a process of self-alienation and suicide. He writes that self-alienation refers to the inability to positively actualize and actively exercise one's personal and cultural gifts. Self-alienation involves a process of being separated from one's real self – that potentially organized and dynamically integrated set of emotional, intellectual, behavioral, social, spiritual and acquired socio-historical skills which, under conducive environmental/social conditions, can be used by the individual to achieve optimal well-being.

Self-alienated people, Wilson writes, are not permitted to be their real selves. They must live for someone or something other than themselves. They live outside themselves. They cannot define themselves but are defined by others. They are externalized; controlled from the outside. They are not centered. Their self-definition, self-satisfaction, self-direction and happiness must be secured from outsiders. They dare not expose themselves or others to their true feelings. Their experiences must be artificially inseminated. Having lost contact with their true feelings, they depend on other people, alienating social rituals and consumption patterns to actualize their alienated existence.

The concept of self-alienation I found to be very helpful to understanding myself. Self-alienation is what I was experiencing as a teen and what I imagine most Black youth in my neighborhood were experiencing. The concept of self-alienation I thought was the main reason why Black on Black crime is perpetuated in our communities. Self-alienation grows out of a sense of self-hatred that in the words of Karen

Horney in her book, *Neurosis and Human Growth* finally culminates in direct self-destructive impulses and actions. These may be acute or chronic, openly violent or insidious and slow grinding, conscious or unconscious, carried out in action or performed in imaginary ways only. They may concern minor or major issues. They aim ultimately at physical, psychic, and spiritual self-destruction.

Black self-hatred leads to emotional and psychological detachment that makes it possible for young Black men to rob and beat up each other, to hurt and oppress each other, and even to murder each another. This had to be the explanation for the culture of violence that existed in the ghetto. All of those murders and gang assaults by Black youth and men against other Blacks had to be driven by this self-hatred. Poverty as the key factor was not convincing enough for me. Not having income could not account for the attitude we had toward other Black boys. The act of violently confronting another Black person in the mind of a Black teenager, makes him feel as though he is confronting himself or that part of himself that he deeply hated and wanted to do away with. In a poem that I wrote soon after my 18th birthday, I raised the questions: What are the symptoms of a traumatized Black boy? Is it uncontrollable rage? Is it melancholy dripping off his skin? Is it Black apathy? Is it Black anarchy? Is it a Black boy holding a nine-millimeter gun to the head of an image that could easily pass as his biological brother?

My experience growing up in the ghetto of Newburgh was continually traumatizing. Everyone was a victim of this trauma. Every day amidst a culture of violence and deep despair was forcing me further into a dark hole of anger and depression. Some Black youth were already there. Most had already begun to replicate the violence that they had digested and were victims of themselves. Others took to drug abuse to escape depression but found themselves digging deeper into depression. In retrospect, I believe that most Black and brown young people in Newburgh existed in the same dark hole of anger and depression. And it was from that dark hole that the majority of us were dying trying to get out. Many of us were dying trying to be something other than Black. What that other thing was has always been beyond my grasp. We weren't trying to become white; and what would that mean anyway? We were just trying to escape our Black bodies since it was the source of our discontent. The history of white racism, overtly and covertly, had taught us that Black skin was a badge of shame and not having a mechanism to counter white racist ideology, we consumed it and became part of it. Black youth then and now are actually devouring themselves in order to exist outside of their own skin. Being Black they believe is the reason why they are poor, why they are in the ghetto, why they are suffering more than any other people.

Black violence begins first in the white assault on the image of the Black body. That is, in other words, Black children interpret their own Blackness through the lens of a white society that has rejected and demonized Blackness. Black children view their own Black skin as attacked and ultimately destroyed through the use of media and the information they receive in school. These negative portrayals that distort and damage Black self-perception enable Black youth to look at other Black youth with disdain and loathing. It is a denial of their own and other youths' Blackness. They see and feel the need to eliminate what they were taught not to love.

CHAPTER 24

MOVING TOO FAST

BY MY 15th birthday I was already feeling that I might end up dead soon. Life was dragging along at a snail's pace and the scene on the streets hadn't changed. It was the day before summer and the temperature was already humid. Black kids were out early, thirsty for some drama to get into. The cops became more consistent in their patrols through the ghetto because their attitude was that the summer heat brought out the violence in Black youth. But it had more to do with the fact that school was out and there were hardly any activities for us, so the streets became our playground and the props of drugs, guns, and reasons to fight were still left over from last summer.

My friends and I would try to predict how many people would be murdered before summer ended. It was like watching a movie in the hood. That's how disconnected we were from it all because none of us were actually ever involved in the killings as the shooter or the victim. And many times the deaths were not so close to home that we had reason to be fearful. There was always daily chatter about so and so getting shot or so and so getting bagged for a body, arrested off the street. My friends and I weren't going to funerals so I at least didn't comprehend the gravity or the consequences of murder. Like moviegoers we felt that it would never be one of us who would end up the victim or the one behind the trigger. That was how it was before I turned 15.

Things seemed much more dreadful than before. I was a little older and better acquainted with the streets. I knew what blocks not to venture on and who to stay away from. My mother was getting tired of me as well. The older I got, the more she said I reminded her of my father, a man who left her with nothing but heartache and three young boys to raise in the heart of the inner-city. The more my adolescent ways became a nuisance to her, the faster she would tell me to leave her house to go become a man out there in the streets. Since my father wasn't man enough to stick around, she wasn't going to allow me to affirm my manhood in a household that she had managed all by herself. So I found myself in the streets a lot, looking for something that I couldn't find at home. I didn't have a dad. I didn't have a hero, someone who I could look up to.

I felt that my mother didn't love me enough and I knew that my ghetto didn't possess a heart big enough to ever love me. So I was lost. I was lost in a concrete wilderness with no direction and with all of the madness happening around me that was now in plain view, I just knew that it was too easy to become a victim out there. Either I was going to fulfill the prophecy of some of my disgruntled teachers who angrily said that I would never see my 20s, or I was going to survive somehow. I didn't have much belief in the latter with all the homicides that were taking place around me. It was all making me crazy and halfway through my 15th year of life I had seen so much street violence that I had to restrain my anger from using my body as a weapon to hurt another Black male trapped in this wilderness.

I was a caged bird screaming to deaf ears. Everyone around could interpret my strange behavior only as adolescent rebellion — acting out is what Black kids do for attention, or this is just a juvenile phase I am going through, is how everyone explained away my unheard screaming. I couldn't fly away although everything about my innate nature begged to escape this cage. And even if the front door was open, where could I go? If I did happen to walk out of my cage, another one awaited me.

I was about to become a teenage father. Mecca, my girlfriend, was pregnant with my child.

I certainly wasn't ready for fatherhood. I looked at fatherhood in the most selfish way possible. My rationale was that just in case I died soon out in the streets, my child, a life that I had made with my own loins, would forever carry a piece of me. That belief played into the psychosis of Black males scrimmaging with death. It was my justification to anyone having anything to say against me becoming a father at such a young age. That and the other reality that I was just a teenager excited by having discovered sex and excited that I was about to finally have someone I could unconditionally love, my own baby who could return a love that I had yet to know and feel. Raising and providing for my child was something that I hadn't even begun to think about. It was all fantasy for Mecca and me. We just assumed that things would be perfect and that we could somehow run away from Newburgh and life would be so much easier elsewhere. I was even pushing myself harder in school to finish, and was hanging less with certain friends on the street corners we frequented.

Six months into Mecca's pregnancy, a sonogram revealed that she was having a girl. I was speechless and overwhelmed. My street diction could not paint a vivid picture for Mecca of what I was feeling when we learned about our baby girl growing inside her. My own father had vanished by the time I turned eight so I didn't have much of a father model to follow, but my feelings told me that I would be the best father I could possibly be to my daughter. I was going to protect her no matter what.

CHAPTER 25

BUYING A GUN

VICTIMIZED PEOPLE punish themselves beyond initial victimization to justify their own paralysis. They become fearful of thought or action to gain empowerment to affect change. Newburgh made many of us its victims. As victims we found ways to victimize others to make them feel our pain. The victim paralysis had set in a long time ago in our ghetto community where no one had the courage or ability to imagine that things could be better or any different. We just accepted things as they were and reacted to every tragic blow as it came. I was no different from any of the homeboys out there in the streets or any different from the people who live in this community. We shared the same hopes and fears because we all existed in the same space and time. So much bonds us as a people and a community, be it a place like Newburgh or our entire Black history in general. The only difference for me was that I wanted to live more than I wanted to die. I didn't want another gun pointed at my head threatening to take away my life. It was that simple. I had had enough and was willing to defend myself rather than be stripped of my manhood by someone trying to rob me of my possessions. It was not that my life was less valuable than a gold chain or a pair of sneakers. It was rather that as a young Black male, this chain or those sneakers were all that I had left. They were my pride and what gave me meaning and I was willing to fight for what was mine just like anyone else out on the streets.

But I refused victimization. I refused the idea of wounded people wanting to hurt others to ease their own suffering. The ghetto became a home for weak predators preying on the weaker and I became frustrated with it all. That frustration and the fear of getting blasted away by someone led me to think that I needed a gun for protection. A gun was the only thing that affirmed a street guy's manhood. It made him appear tough and strengthened his standing in the streets. People thought twice about testing him if they believed that he was a shooter. A decade before it was all about fisticuffs but that soon became obsolete. My generation had graduated to the use of handguns to settle disputes and guns were easily accessible now that drugs were eating away at our community.

For the past ten years or so I've asked myself over and over again, was my decision to protect myself with a gun the best decision? Under the deadly circumstances I was living in, I kept concluding that I did not want to die. That required a gun. That is my truth. It does not condone or justify anything.

I can't make sense of the deep madness that exists in my ghetto streets, and how it sometimes robs you of your human ability to act rationally. Sometimes all the rules are thrown out the window and paranoia drives you into illegal acts that you rationalize to be just and necessary. The law, you know, is suspended in the jungle. So your wrong is right and your right is wrong. And everything becomes justified and rationalized as just another act of survival. The prospect of death is always real, in any hood. Death always felt like it was just around the corner. How could we resist death other than by getting our hands around a firearm and being willing to shoot back or shoot first to avoid being shot dead?

Getting my hands on a gun was too easy. If you had the money, someone was always willing to sell you a gun. They don't ask questions or do background checks. They just take your money and give you what they have. The word around town was that a guy by the name of Big Lize was selling guns. He was an older guy from the Dark Side gang that occupied the block where I lived. I knew of Big Lize but I didn't know him personally. He was a tall dark skinned dude with humongous hands and gold rings around each of his fingers, but not on his thumbs. When I approached him about getting a gun, it was apparent that I could have been his little brother or nephew. The only thing I remember him asking me was whether I knew how to use a gun and if I had the money to pay for it. I handed over $40 bucks and he passed me a palm-sized handgun and told me to put it away. I tucked the gun away in my waistband and covered it with my jacket and then left the hallway where we made that quick fatal transaction.

I didn't carry the gun every day and I never brought it to school. My only fears were my mother catching me, or having my little brothers see it and tell on me. So I would carry it only at night when I had to walk the streets. When I came home I would leave it in the backyard at the bottom of a trashcan. It was safer there than being in my house where anyone could find it.

CHAPTER 26

FATAL SHOOTING

ACROSS THE street from my girlfriend Mecca's house were some older guys who would hang out in front of an apartment building, smoking and drinking and occasionally blasting music from the radio in one of their parked cars. They were way older, but one of the guys—his name was Victor—I had known because I was a friend of his cousin Orlando before he moved back to New Jersey. There was never any beef between me and Victor's crew because they knew that I was a younger dude who was always on the block visiting my girlfriend and they were more into getting drunk than into street drama. Everything changed once Victor introduced me to his cousin Germaine called "G" who had arrived from Fort Lauderdale, Florida, sometime in April or May of 1996.

"G" and I exchanged a few words, nothing more than a "What's up" and a handshake. We were from two different worlds as far as I was concerned. He was from the South and I was from Newburgh, New York. I was 15 and he was 18. That was the first time I met "G" and then I hadn't seen him in a few weeks. The next time I ran into him was near the apartment where Victor and his crew hung out. I was sitting on the front porch of Mecca's house when "G" called me from across the street where he was standing. I walked over there thinking that everything was cool between us and for the most part everything was. "G" asked me *"Was I banging?"* and I really didn't know what he meant by that so I was taken a little off guard. Then he asked me if I was *"Dame* (Swahili for blood)*"* or a Blood gang member and if *"I was banging on Crips or Folk?"* At that time there were not any Crips or Folk in Newburgh, so I had never met a Folk personally. (Folk or Folk Nation is an alliance of gangs such as The Gangster Desciples and the Crips.) He assumed I was a Blood because he noticed that I wore the color red a lot, which I did because red was my favorite color. The first and only Blood I had known at that time was my friend Dre but I hadn't seen him in over three years and my so called gang phase happened when I was 13 and probably ended around the same time because the national gang culture of the Bloods and the Crips was never indigenous to Newburgh despite all the crews and wannabe gangs that existed and tried to exist on Newburgh's streets. Whether I had answered his questions or not, "G" was adamant about showing off his tattoos to me in an attempt to intimidate me. With his T-shirt now off, he began to brag about every gang tattoo that was engraved into his body. It was like he was celebrating having earned every needle and ink stroke that formed the symbols that found their home on his flesh. His tattoos represented his journey through gang life. They were evidence of his being a banger and his way of telling me that I had better never cross the line. I don't remember saying much in response to him describing his Folk tattoos. When he was done talking, his monologue ended and we went our separate ways.

The next time we crossed paths happened to be in a dark alley on Lutheran Street. I was at Mecca's house all day and by nightfall I decided to walk home. As I strolled down the block someone yoked me from behind and pressed a cold gun into my right jawline. I knew that I was being robbed and mad that I didn't have my gun with me to defend myself in this vulnerable situation. I didn't resist or do anything. I just stood there with my eyes closed and then I was spun around so that I stood face to face with the person holding the gun to my head. It was "G" and he chuckled as if it was all a joke. He seemed to be under the influence of drugs. And before I walked off both frightened and angered, he didn't hesitate to remind that I better watch my back out here. From then on I wasn't leaving home without my gun on me.

The last time I saw "G" alive was on June 17, 1996. It was around 11:30 at night and the streets were already dark and empty. Mecca and I had decided to leave her house and walk to my house several blocks away down on the Dark Side. By the time we had reached the middle of the block, a voice from the opposite side of the street was calling Mecca's name. The voice was coming from the shadows on the other side of the street. At first we didn't recognize the voice or see anyone. We were both startled for a few seconds and then someone was running towards us. It was "G." Something about him was not right; he was not acting normal. His eyes seemed possessed by an inhuman force, perhaps cocaine or PCP because he was extremely hyperactive and threatening. Mecca and I both knew "G" and I had a few encounters with him over the past few weeks but I never assumed that there was a serious problem between us. He must have felt otherwise because as Mecca and I were walking away, he continued to approach us, intimidating us with his frenzied body movements and verbal threats. I didn't understand him or know what had happened that made him so enraged. He seemed to be under the influence of the drugs he sold. He was screaming at the top of his lungs, screaming that I better get the fuck out of here before he kills me and that he didn't know what I was doing around here. His screaming shut out any other sound on that dark street. All you could hear was "G's" yells. They were bringing people to their front windows to find out what was going on in the street. They clearly saw a conflict out on the street but no one came out to break it up or to help us. I tried to walk away but he kept running in front of me, provoking me to respond to his craziness.

Mecca's father also heard the screams and came outside and

recognized his daughter and me in some kind of trouble up the block. He grabbed me, pulling me away from "G" in an attempt to stop the emotionally charged fracas that was going on. But "G" kept coming, yelling in the face of Mecca's father then back in my face. Then "G" grabbed hold of Mecca's arm aggressively. She tried to pull away but he grabbed tighter and refused to let go. They struggled and then I saw Mecca fall to the ground with such violence that her father let go of me in shock. "G" was over her, his body pinning her against the ground. Everything seemed to have happened in one sweeping motion. I lost myself in the fear that Mecca and my unborn child that she was carrying were hurt. My only concern was her and my unborn.

Mecca was still on the ground. She lay there unconscious as a result of smacking her head against the pavement. I tried to pull her up and away from "G" who was still in the way and holding on to her. Things were happening so fast in those few intense minutes. A surreal darkness, other than the already dark night sky and dimly lit street, engulfed us. I panicked and lost my self-control. I'm not sure that "G" and I exchanged any further words after that. I just don't remember. The only thing I could see in the darkness was Mecca on the ground and "G" on top of her. He refused to let her go. And then I saw him struggling with an object in his pocket. I couldn't tell if it was a gun or a knife or something else. I didn't wait to see him pull whatever it was from his pocket. In one swift motion I pulled out my own gun and fired two shots. I missed him completely, and did not find out until I was arrested that one bullet ricocheted off the cement sidewalk and struck the carotid artery in "G's" neck.

CHAPTER 27

UNDERSTANDING SELF HATE

HARLEM VALLEY had the reputation of being the most dangerous juvenile housing facility in New York State. Black and Latino youth made up the majority of the population. Many of them belonged to a street gang. Almost everyone came from an urban community in one of the five boroughs of New York City. Broken homes, drug abuse, negligence and crime, were all part of the grim story that connected us in one way or another.

During our daily one-hour group sessions, violence was a constant theme that kept coming up. Every one of us had been affected by violence. Growing up in the ghetto in the culture of violence taught us how to be violent and how to hurt other people.

The gang presence at the Valley constituted young Black and brown teenagers united by the need for a sense of belonging and for protection. They would form pocket associations to protect one another while incarcerated. These gangs, although prohibited from being formed and belonging to them, acted as protection against the vulnerability of a young prisoner getting jumped or extorted by others. Once a teen joins a gang, he is expected to live by the gang's code of conduct and to always defend his gang family. This meant that there was always tension in the Valley. It was not uncommon for fights to happen every day, and for someone to get stabbed. It was the inevitable daily result whenever two rival gangs shared the same space. Lock up was really not very different from the streets. It had the same exhibition of violence and conflict, only now a lot more concentrated.

That same street mentality of trying to get over on the weak and looking for prey to exercise your frustrations flowed through Harlem Valley. From the first time I stepped foot on the unit where I would be housed and had the gaze of 20 or so other young men focused on my fresh-to-the-system face, my fear and expectations of the unknown wrestled with my rational search for the truth about my new situation. What did I get myself into? Will I have to fight to prove myself? How will I survive in this place? Many questions came into my head one after the other. At 16 years old and in jail for killing someone, I was no longer oblivious to the personal devastation that violence can create. My own life showed clearly what acts of violence can lead to. There was also a sensible part of me that realized that it was a great shame that young Black and brown men were at odds with one another over virtually nothing and more than prepared to take each other out for no good reason at all.

Over the course of several years in juvenile lock up, I would see first-hand the great amount of emotional and psychological energy that most of these young incarcerated brothers expended in the spirit of violence. Violence was such a daily experience among us that we were victims of it more than anything else. We were consumed by it. It was perhaps the only language we understood. But that language and the behavior that accompanied it, was created by generations before us that lacked the love necessary to heal their own pain and suffered from the kind of brutality that could be born only out of hatred.

It was difficult trying to maintain a clean record in jail among kids who had a thing for creating havoc on the unit. The administrators would do their best to separate rival gangs from one another but at times when residents did not identify themselves to the administration about their gang affiliations, a Crip or Latin King would end up on a unit housing Bloods and a riot would break out. Although I was already associated with the Bloods from my connection to my friend Dre back home, I wasn't willing to join a gang in lock up because it had negative consequences and could damage the appeal of my case. Besides, gangs in jail were mainly for the purpose of self-protection, and knowing that a gang had your back always meant that some knuckle head would exploit that and cause unnecessary problems on the unit. Because I was reading certain Black authors at the time and trying to figure out my own identity for the first time, I was more interested in discovering ways to share my new insights with the others. We all had the same problems, and came from similar neighborhoods, so I imagined that my developing consciousness and the strong Black language I was learning should unify us rather than divide us. At this point of our incarceration, we were all here because we had inflicted harm upon our communities and now the only thing separating us was a red or blue or yellow gang flag.

CHAPTER 28

BEYOND THE GANG FLAG

ONE DAY during our group discussion I was asked my thoughts about human nature and whether I believed that young Black males in particular have a proclivity to violence and nihilistic patterns. Our discussion was spawned by the topic of how the media uses negative hyperbole to describe Black defendants. We were passing around an old news article concerning the five young men who were accused and convicted of raping a white woman in Central Park in the late 1980s. That crime had received much media coverage and it had perpetuated the post-slavery idea that Black males are innately predisposed to monstrous acts of brutality towards themselves and others. My answer was that I believed people were innately good and positive, that they strived towards the betterment of self or family or tribe or village. I imagined that people generally possessed the desire to do what was right in accordance with their own morality and spirituality. Having to choose between good or evil, I think most people would naturally gravitate towards good and refrain from doing evil acts that conflict with their understanding of right action and justice.

But at the same time, after being around other youth in this confinement, I understood how the absence of an infrastructure that promoted positive cultural values and morality could allow negative experiences and bad information to corrupt the moral conscience of individuals and groups. Negative information, especially if reinforced by destructive cultural forces, could shape our attitudes and ultimately our behavior. What are we thinking and feeling about ourselves and about others who look like us, and how do we feel about people who don't look like us or share our common experience? Where do we learn negative concepts and who reinforces them? Who benefits from them and how does the acceptance of these concepts happen; who is affected and who profits? I was always thinking deeply about these questions and I always had profound answers to give to my group. I wanted the others to think critically about their lives and the environment around them.

Our group discussions were hardly ever conclusive. We rarely seemed to reach any concrete answers and none of the conclusions that we did reach were ever going to justify our crimes or free us from prison. We were more interested in providing historical context for our lives and understanding how we used to live. We wanted to become more than a name and a state prison identification number. We were more than a summary of the crimes we committed along with the New York State Penal Code statutes that defined our offenses. We were still human. Most of us wanted to hold on to what was left of our humanity, even after it had been debased, put on trial and convicted.

We never focused on anyone's actual convictions. That was personal information that no one was forced to disclose. But we did focus on the motivations of our crimes and the causes of our being sent to prison. It was understood that many of our petty crimes didn't have to be committed. We were victims of our own youth and ignorance and had no idea of the consequences of our actions. Petty crime was a rite of passage for us. It was our way of proving our maleness to one another. It had very little to do with disrupting social order. However these same petty crimes evolved into more serious crimes, and they became our way of life until prison stopped us in our tracks. Now we had to confront the reality of a victimization that was predatory and reciprocal in nature. In the wrecking of our own communities, we had destroyed our own already fragile youth and were now self-studied specimens inside a prison we called the Belly of the Beast. Blind rage and anger that was bone deep, without knowledge of its source, had colored our lives for way too long. When we were on the outside, we were far from free. In fact, we were born prisoners already. We were prisoners of an urban Black experience that wrought nothing life giving. Life was supposed to beget life but instead the whole culture around us begot only death. And death always came too soon. The brutal New York winters killed us. The hot summers killed us. The police killed us. Rival gangs killed us. The crack culture that transformed men and woman into mindless and spineless characters of disrespect and Black failure before the eyes of my generation killed our hopes and dreams of ever becoming something more than drug dealers.

As ironic as it sounds, being in prison made us feel free in ways that the streets never made us feel free. The barbed wire fences and electronic doors were just that and the prison rules still restricted us and reminded us daily that we were far from running wild in the streets of our old neighborhoods. It was the fact that this new environment didn't rob us or threaten to snatch away our lives that brought us a calm that many of us never knew before. Yeah, we couldn't wear our street clothing or have possession of anything from the outside or to come and go as we pleased. But our bodies were now free; imprisoned, yes! But free from the flesh tearing bullets and knives that were our former reality. Our bodies were now covered in the same prison uniform that made us equal in appearance. We still had our differences like our tribal allegiances or the particular neighborhoods that we came from, but in essence we knew that we were all the same now. We all had one fate and shared one destiny and that was to find ourselves for the very first time with nothing but time on our hands.

Once I got adjusted to my new prison life at Harlem Valley, and established my position outside the gang culture of violence, I began to feel that I was in a safe place for the first time since I felt safe at home with my mother when I was six years old.

CHAPTER 29

EDUCARE, PULLING FROM WITHIN

EVER SINCE I knew Margaret, she insisted that I read literature and that I make education a big part of my life. I was incarcerated now and facing a very long sentence, nine years to life. When everything around me in the confines of prison was telling me to give up hope, Margaret was there encouraging me to educate myself and never to give up my humanity to the Prison System. She would remind me of the story of the once enslaved Frederick Douglas and how his determination to learn how to read ultimately paved the way not only to his own freedom but also to the abolition of slavery altogether. Margaret wrote letters to me as much as possible and periodically sent me post cards from her travels around the world. Her letters were always inspiring and were written in a spirit of hope and love. She always spoke optimistically for she believed that prison was just the beginning of my story and not the end. She insisted that I devote myself to self-education and she consistently sent me book after book until I had developed a passion for reading.

Reading was my escape from the barbarism of prison. Both the other prisoners and the guards were slaves to the mechanisms of prison. The guards did everything they could to make our time in prison hell, dehumanizing prisoners at will, threatening to throw rebellious prisoners into solitary confinement, or taking them to private sections of the prison to beat them up. The adult prison system was a much more hardened place than the juvenile facility I spent five years in before being sent to adult corrections at 21. Prisoners had to pretend to be harder than they were to climb up the hierarchy that existed on the inside. No one wanted to appear weak for that made you vulnerable to other prisoners. So prison psychology became a game of survival and dodging the guards to make life a little easier. I did what I had to do to survive in there and stayed away from the guards as much as possible. But I found my solitude and peace in practices such as Buddhism and the study of Islam and adopted a vegan diet just to avoid the processed foods served by the prison.

I learned that Education was a word derived from the Latin roots, *'educo'* and *'educare,'* which means to pull out from within. If the pursuit of education was to obtain knowledge then the most resourceful and rewarding knowledge was *knowledge of self*. My prior experience in school was the exact opposite of what I knew now about the education process. Schools were an institution that took away freedom of thought from students and assumed that they possessed no real knowledge of any value. So they waste the most critical years of a student's life depositing useless information into the students' brains and teaching them *what to think and not how to think* in a critical and constructive way. The literature that Margaret was sending me, mostly biographies and classical subjects that were totally skipped over by my former schools, was introducing me to characters who carved out their own freedom despite concentration camps, slave plantations or prisons in which these strong characters found themselves incarcerated.

Since I was 15 when I came into the prison system, I missed my opportunity to graduate from high school. But Margaret thought it a good idea that I go back to school while still in the County Jail awaiting my trial. I did so as a good way to keep busy and ended up receiving my high school GED at 16 before I went to Harlem Valley Secure Center.

Like any other prisoner, I faced many challenges trying to adjust to a new world. But once I learned the ropes of the System, doing time was just that; I had to learn to do the time and not let the time do me in. Before I knew it I was a leader rather than a follower in prison. I had discovered that reading gave me a freedom that no judge or prison warden could ever offer me. Reading freed my mind and I wanted others to experience what I was now learning. I became an advocate of education while in prison, passing books along to anyone who was interested in reading, and always willing to teach fellow Black prisoners a form of knowledge of self where they could begin to connect with the larger world beyond the small neighborhood or block they were from. It was all about raising consciousness in the prisoner. Transform their thinking and you transform their behavior, and then the communities they came from and will ultimately return to may also be transformed. The empowered prisoner, I believed, is obligated to bring something back to the community from which he was taken.

At times I was successful at convening rival gangs in a discussion where we explored the idea of urban genocide. Black youth were at war with one another, killing each other over gang colors, and many of the youth I encountered in prison were victims of this urban war. Our discussions changed their outlook on life and although they may not have returned to their communities to become activists, they certainly brought a level of mutual respect and peace between rival gangs in our prison. Things were calm enough in the Valley for the administration to agree to start a pilot college program that Margaret and her husband Peter Stern managed to start for qualified residents. (Peter Stern was chairman of the Storm King Art Center sculpture park south of Newburgh for 50 years.) This program allowed me and other youth to earn college credits while still incarcerated. This was an academic opportunity that most of us would never have been exposed to if we were still on the outside. To participate in the college program we first had to obtain our GED and then maintain good conduct. Any troubles would forfeit our chances of being in the college program. So the facility was better off having residents committed to education than to be engaged in riots where both the residents and the staff were at risk of getting injured.

Finally, for the first time in our lives, we young men were striving to improve ourselves through something worthwhile like attending college. It gave us all a real sense of purpose and meaning in our lives after our schools had failed us. The college program at the Valley was a success. In our first semester every enrolled student successfully completed all of his classes. The facility celebrated our accomplishment by allowing the students to have a Family Day Festival where our families could spend an entire day with us and we could enjoy our favorite foods from the outside.

The professors who Dutchess Community College offered were brave for stepping foot inside a juvenile prison, and even more courageous for trying to get through to a group of teenagers the System had deemed unfit for society. They cared about us and believed that prison did not have to define who we were. The curriculum combined with how the professors interacted with us added a colorful combination of compassion, consciousness raising and empathy for the challenges that each student personally faced.

When I was not studying and doing college work, I was painting and showing off my work to other residents and staff. Eventually, many staff enjoyed my art and the prison's administration allowed me to have an exhibit in the facility's visiting room and I was even allowed to sell a few paintings. By 2001 I had amassed a large enough collection of art so that Margaret decided to enter two of my pastel paintings in my first juried art show at Mount Saint Mary's College *Annual Artists on the Campus* art show. My incarceration prevented me from attending the art show but my family and friends attended and I won second place for my *"Mother and Son"* pastel portrait.

A short time after my first show, I also participated in another juried show held by the Orange County Art Federation at the Brotherhood Winery in Washingtonville, NY. There I submitted my pastel painting, *"The Saxophone Player,"* a tribute to the late saxophonist John Coltrane in dark hues of grays and black. I received a Best in Show Award for this painting. I had two awards in my first two professional shows. I was feeling really confident and proud of myself for getting recognition for my art while in prison. The following year I had my own one-man exhibition of paintings at the Newburgh Free Library during Black History Month. Fifty of my paintings were on public display for the entire month. Through my art I returned to Newburgh to let my old neighborhood know that I was still alive and making the best of life in prison. The Newburgh Free Library show and my prior two awards helped me to become a member of the Kent Art Association and the Middletown Art Group while still behind bars.

Painting and my pursuit of education while in prison were positive forces giving me hope of a better life someday, in spite of being locked up in jail for I knew not how long.

CHAPTER 30

GERMAINE

It is hard not to think about Germaine. I have thought about him since the night of our tragic confrontation. Many nights I have tried to erase him and that night from my memory, but I could not. Something that life changing can't be easily removed from memory. Part of me has grown to accept the fact that he is now and forever part of my life. Everything that he was and all that I knew of him—not much beyond his drug dealing and his blatant Crip and Folk gang tattoos—is painfully etched into my mind. I hardly knew him, so things such as his laughter or even the contours of his face have escaped my memory. The fact that I could find it so easy to erase a man who once lived; to minimize his existence to some damn gang tattoos scares me. I totally get the metaphor in all of this. To kill a Black brother, and my only remaining memory of him is his Black body and tattoos, how can I look at myself and not feel that I killed myself? I was no different from white cops who kill unarmed Black men, except for the fact that every time I looked into a mirror I faced the guilt of killing one of my own kind.

Faint memories or not, Germaine is part of every breath I take. Although it feels impersonal I still feel obliged to carry him with me. Taking a life is a selfish act; I don't ever want to forget that because of my self-defense actions on that dreadful night Germaine could never experience life again.

Intellectual and emotional growth has helped me become a better and wiser person. Today I can look beyond the circumstances of that night and see the meaning of that experience. Germaine and I were driven by hate on that night. I don't know why he hated me. I hated the idea that I was being confronted by him on my neighborhood block where I always hung out. I hated that he had the nerve to question my manhood. I hated that Mecca and I were being threatened. But in the end, regardless of what I once thought about Germaine, I carry the weight of his soul upon my conscience. It is an enormous burden. I carry it because I know that Germaine had to be more than the man I killed on that tragic night. He was a son, a grandson, a nephew, a cousin, a brother. You never know what impact one death has and how far reaching it is until after the fact. We are not in this universe alone. We share this space with so many people and are interconnected to others in so many ways that our death disrupts the balance of their galaxies. So I accept the awful fact that I robbed Germaine's entire family. His attacking me and my using a gun made us mortal enemies long enough for me to snatch away the dreams and hopes a mother and father had for their son.

I own that. I own what I did. I own what I have done to his family and to my own family. Years and years of reflection and growth have humbled me, and that humility has always brought me to question my character and the meaning of my actions. Had that night not been written into the script of our lives, what could Germaine and I have become? I will never know the answer to that question. Here and now we are dying due to gang banging or police brutality, and not once do we ponder how life could be so different if death had not eliminated so many of us. With these thoughts I carry the weight of Germaine's death with me every day.

CHAPTER 31

MY TRIAL BEGINS

AFTER MY indictment for murder when I was 15, I was sent to Valhalla Juvenile Detention Center in Westchester County. It was June of 1996. Although I was too young to be sent to the Orange County Jail with adult offenders, the law allowed me to be charged with a crime as an adult. Juveniles like myself were being charged as adults for certain crimes due to 2,000 reported crimes allegedly committed by a single youth named Willie Bostic. Bostic was a New York City teen who became infamous within the penal system for committing so many crimes, including at least two subway killings, that authorities finally decided to change the law so that extremely violent offenders such as Willie Bostic could be sentenced to much longer jail terms instead of being sent to a Boys Home and returning back into society when they turn 21. Bostic's rap sheet of offenses was so lengthy that the courts ended up giving him a life sentence without the possibility of ever getting out of prison. I was no Willie Bostic, but just knowing that my juvenile actions could be associated with his history of violence and delinquency made me realize that what I did, and the situation I found myself in, created serious trouble for me.

The first time I was locked inside a cage was in the Goshen detention center for juveniles. I felt that society saw me as an animal, as if I was a danger to the world. I was still a scrawny teenager, weighing no more than 130 pounds, if that. I was only 15 years old. I still couldn't accept the reality that I was being charged with murder. No bone in my body had wanted Germaine dead. I knew that death was permanent, final, an act that could not be undone. Only a few hours separated me from the shooting and I still felt shaken up by the whole ordeal. The last thing I remembered was firing my gun into the darkness in self-defense against a drug dealer attacking me and my pregnant girlfriend.

The holding cell they put me in right after my arrest had a dim light hovering above me. I was in the cell alone and I didn't sense that anyone was near me in adjacent cells because there were no familiar human sounds other than the static from a police radio going off every few seconds somewhere in the distance. My mind was constantly racing back and forth and I couldn't sleep. The shooting replayed and replayed and replayed over and over again in my mind. Did I kill him? Did I seriously injure him? Was my girlfriend injured? Those thoughts and the after effects of a traumatic experience that had just occurred hours ago – body shaking, cold sweat, nervousness, anxiety and fear – kept me from sleeping. My mind and body refused to settle for the night.

Almost every day I was being escorted before a judge and back to the detention facility by State Troopers. Having no understanding of legal procedures, I was absolutely lost in the courtroom. I had no idea what was being said between the judge and the lawyers or what was going to happen to me. Being vulnerable made me realize how powerless I was. I understood that my own life was no longer in my control, but unfortunately, in the control of people who didn't know me.

Germaine was dead. Mecca had suffered a miscarriage from being attacked by Germaine. I was arrested several hours after the shooting, suspended in a kind of unreal world with no control over what would happen next. I assumed that the authorities would understand my story. They would put the pieces together and see that I was obviously defending my girlfriend and myself. They had to see that continual abuse, harassment and attacks by Germaine led to this unavoidable tragedy. They had to recognize that I was provoked to a point where rational thinking ceases. They would see that the threat to my life was imminent, that the threat to my pregnant girlfriend was real, and that I had to defend her. They had to understand. They had to see my story. I had no other choice but to protect my girlfriend. She was carrying my unborn child. What man wouldn't protect his woman? How did that make me a murderer?

Things didn't happen the way that I thought they should, and the court didn't see things the way I experienced them. In about a week I was indicted before a Grand Jury and charged with Murder in the Second Degree and Criminal Possession of a Weapon in the Third Degree. My heart stopped when I heard what I was being charged with. Why me? Why a murder charge? I was only trying to protect my pregnant girlfriend and myself. Murder! Germaine had confronted and threatened us. Murder! Was he really dead? Murder! I feared losing my own life. "The People are in all respects ready for trial."

During the next few months I found myself bouncing from procedure to procedure, one hearing after another, from the detention facility to court. This was the process before my trial. There were Rosario hearings, Sandoval hearings, a bunch of other pre-trial hearings, and then, "voir dire" or jury selection. With every day getting closer to my trial, my case was in the local newspaper. "Thug Kills." "Gangster Murders." "Gang Feud Turned Deadly." I was found guilty even before my trial began. The media was making me out to be the bad guy, the monster, the aggressor, a gang member. People read the local newspaper. My jury will have read the local newspaper. They will be influenced by what they read. They will find me guilty because of what they read. I will be sent off to rot in prison because the jury will be influenced by what they read in the newspaper. My mind raced back and forth and forth and back. I was hoping for a fair trial. I was hoping for fairness and justice, just once in my life. My story had to be heard. Those responsible for judging my life had to try to walk in my shoes, just for one moment. That's all. Fairness and justice, that's all I was asking for. Yes, I killed Germaine but I was not the aggressor. It was self-defense. I didn't intend to kill him. I had no idea that I actually shot him. I just fired into the darkness, trying to hit his shoulder and stop his attack, not to kill him. With fatally bad luck for "G" and me, the bullet ricocheted off the cement sidewalk and hit his carotid artery.

My trial began six months after the shooting. By that time my 16th birthday came around and I was sent to the County Jail with the adult prisoners. Moving me from the detention facility to the County Jail was convenient for the court since the jail was across the street from the courthouse in Goshen, the Orange County government center.

Trials are a strange experience. It felt like court procedures and the letter of the law as they call it, are more important than the human being, the subject of the Court proceedings.

I hate trials. I hated my trial. It was yet another objectified spectacle that satisfied the performers in the court and in the newspapers. The trial wasn't about what led up to the shooting, or why I had a gun in the first place, or why Germaine, a purported Folk gang member, was making threats against my life on that night. On one hand, it seemed like another one of those perfunctory procedures that I am not really a part of. On the other hand, though it is an abstract process, you know that your life is on the line and you could possibly be thrown away behind bars for a long time.

My trial began. All I remember was a barrage of legal jargon and both attorneys periodically yelling out "Objection" and the judge responding with "Sustained" or "Both Counsels please approach the bench." All I did was sit there at the defendant's table and watch my public defender attorney and the prosecutor perform and try to retell a story that only I knew firsthand. I was a spectator at my own trial. In no way did I feel part of the proceedings. I had no voice, no say in my own trial and in my own life at that moment.

The District Attorney's name in my case was Christopher Boreck. He was a young white prosecutor, probably in his early thirties. When not crying out to the judge about everything that my lawyer attempted to reduce my charge, he would call witness after witness to testify against me. Most of his witnesses were not there on the night of the shooting to witness anything. I would find out later that's how criminal trials are conducted sometimes. Prosecutors would sometimes put questionable witnesses on the stand to describe things they actually never saw just to seal a conviction. But, to my surprise and perhaps the District Attorney's as well, all of the witnesses called by my lawyer would testify to the facts of that night truthfully. Nasihah and his girlfriend were confronted by an older youth on a dark and vacant Newburgh street. It was raining out. There wasn't a crowd of onlookers. Neighbors in their houses heard loud screaming, threats made, the struggling of bodies, tension, people falling, Blackness, gunshots, and people running. Germaine was the aggressor. Nasihah defended his pregnant girlfriend, Mecca. Germaine was the aggressor. Nasihah defended his pregnant girlfriend.

He shot at Germaine's shoulder to stop him, not to kill him. The bullet missed Germaine's body, ricocheted off the cement sidewalk and struck Germaine in his carotid artery. Testimony after testimony told the same story. The District Attorney's direct examinations and my attorney's cross-examination of the witnesses would go on for about two weeks.

The trial seemed to be going in my favor; at least that is what my attorney, Paul Trachte, was telling me. But I knew better. I knew that there was no real way to tell. Everything was in the hands of the jury. They were all white. Germaine was Black and a gangbanger as indicated by his tattoos that were submitted into evidence and I was being portrayed as a rival gang member with an illegal firearm. The jurors didn't know me. The court didn't allow for the jurors to know the real me. I was more than that tragic night. I wasn't looking for trouble. Trouble found me. Trouble found me and I didn't want to die. Contrary to how I had things mapped out in my memory, what the jurors saw was one Black kid from the ghetto of Newburgh who was on trial for killing another Black kid. That is what I was reduced to. I was nothing more. I was not a young teenager. I was not a human being who unfortunately grew up in one of the worst urban Black communities in America. I became everything that is wrong with the ghetto. I became an example of what the murderous streets of Newburgh produce. In contrast to how the District Attorney portrayed me and made me the symbol of Black crime in Newburgh, the jurors pictured Newburgh as a once prosperous and productive city and tourist retreat. Newburgh was now in ruins and plagued with crime, despair, and destruction because of young Black kids like me. The jurors who were all white, middle aged, working class citizens, and far removed from urban Blacks and the reality that we were subjected to, were not a jury of my peers. They didn't know what it was like to walk in my shoes. They couldn't imagine the fear that I had lived with every day inside the ghetto. But they were to judge me and decide my future.

I remember the late rapper and thespian Tupac Shakur when he talked in an interview about having the same fears that white people have, saying that Blacks share the same fears about having a good home, good job, good health, a loving family. But my jurors, my judges did not understand me, a young poor Black kid from the ghetto. I don't have the answers to any of the problems in my ghetto or the resources to fix them. I can't escape my own problems nor everyone else's ghetto problems. So how can an all-white jury begin to understand what it feels like to live next door to a rapist or a robber or a drug dealer or a banger? They couldn't fathom a world of crack heads and junkies and people who will rob a teenager just because they don't have anything. They couldn't imagine how cops could make me understand at a young age that my Black skin was a target of The Law. The cops hunt us our whole lives. And we spend our whole lives running from the police and having to guard ourselves from people who look just like us. Of all the potential jurors in the jury pool, by chance 12 white jurors were the ones ordered to make sense of the terror and pain of a Black boy who was a constant victim of violence. They had to decide whether I was a murderer or if I had acted in self-defense. Because my attorney agreed that they could never truly empathize with me, he believed that it was my best bet to take the stand and to tell my own story of what had occurred that fatal night.

Since the burden of proof was on the State, I did not have to testify, even on my own behalf. I think that was a Fifth Amendment issue against self-incrimination but I was not willing to risk my life on the Constitution that I didn't respect as totally fair in the first place. This was my life on trial and I knew the prosecution's witnesses were not at the shooting, were not accurate or fair. I knew that I had to tell my side of the story whether the judge and the jury believed me or not.

Sitting on the witness seat I felt like I was lab specimen being studied. All eyes were on me. The eyes of a courtroom full of white people were staring me up and down. The feeling in itself was overwhelming. I literally felt like a black dot in a sea of whiteness. All of my limbs felt fettered, chained and shackled and at one point during my own testimony, I felt like my limbs were amputated. I felt this foreign feeling once before, when a cop had placed handcuffs tightly around my wrists. I felt limbless and a kind of disconnect that I really cannot put clearly into words. I was not in possession of my own body. I was present but I was outside of my own flesh. My body was on trial and I was an abstract voice disconnected from it, and somehow made to tell my story of its journey to ears that couldn't fully understand without having walked in my shoes.

On the day that I took the stand to testify for myself, the State Troopers came early that morning to escort me from jail to the

Courthouse. I was dressed in an olive colored suit and tie. This was the first time I ever wore a suit. Not even when going to church as a kid did I have to wear a dress suit. My attorney wanted me to look as presentable as possible to the jurors, as non-threatening to them as possible. He even advised me to cut off my hair. I didn't understand how my cornrow braids posed a threat to white jurors but he insisted they did. So my braids were traded in for a cropped haircut. I was as presentable as I could get, short of magically transforming my skin color. I was brought into the courtroom where my trial was going on, the same room I found myself in for the past two weeks as a spectator watching my defense attorney and the District Attorney toss my life around like a football.

The courtroom was nearly empty except for my attorney and the District Attorney standing at their tables. I was escorted over to my table next to my lawyer and sat down beside him without really paying any attention to him. He asked if I was ready. I was as ready as I could get. "Get focused!" he said. Get focused? How could I not be focused when it was my life that was on trial and I was being tried for murder? I was being tried for killing a man, a man who attacked my pregnant girlfriend and who threatened to kill me, a man who had been telling people that he was going to stab me in my stomach and kill me, and then shows up late at night on a dark street erratic and out of control, making the same threats and then slamming my pregnant girlfriend to the ground. So I shoot. I didn't want to but I did. It all happened so fast. He reached for something underneath his shirt. I didn't know if he had a gun, or a knife, or no weapon. So I fired. I fired my gun to stop him from attacking and I ended up causing the death of Germaine. I killed him. I killed another human being. I didn't want him to kill me first. That's self-defense. I tell my attorney that I am as focused and as ready as I will ever be.

After about ten minutes the courtroom began to fill. I am sure that some of the people who began to fill the seats behind me were my family and friends but I am trying to be focused and not look behind me. I am trying not to be distracted. I kept telling myself not to be concerned with anything around me, just block everything out. I'm focused, with my eyes staring straight ahead of me, penetrating the sign above the judge's head that reads, "In God We Trust." In God We Trust, American Flag, A Courtroom, Old White Judge and All White Jurors. How did I allow myself to get in this position? My life was on trial and I was about to be judged by a courtroom of people who didn't know me. They couldn't understand what it was like growing up in a place like Newburgh. They didn't come from my world. They were on the outside trying to look into a world that was dark and violent and everything that the larger society was not. I began to tell myself that there was no way that I could win this trial. White jurors could never understand the madness that rips at the root of what could be a good quality of life in the ghetto. If they are responsible for judging me, how could they learn the context of the environment that I came from if my trial wasn't about the bigger picture? It wasn't about my whole life in the ghetto. It was simply about that night and how I fired a handgun that took the life of Germaine.

In God We Trust. The American Flag. A Courtroom. Old White Judge and All White Jurors. Gangs. Drug Territories. Deadly Shootouts and gunshots ringing through the ghetto night. Crime. Robberies. Gang assaults. Jumped. Chased home. Harassed. Attacked. Threatened. Fear. Terror. Hatred. Hatred. Hatred. Rage. Rage. Rage. Anger. Anger. Anger. Running home. Followed. Scared. Imprisoned in my own home. Terror. Terror. Terror. Gang shootouts. Stabbings. Run. Run. Run. Wrong block. Wrong time. Wrong color. No Where To Run. No Where To Hide. Fear. React. Fear. React. I shoot. I shoot in fear. I shoot to save my life. Arrested for Murder. In God We Trust and I am on trial for having defended my life and for taking the life of another youth. All of these emotions became bullet points in my head, playing over and over, reminding me of all that I suffered growing up in my home city.

The court officer walked into the courtroom and told everyone present to please rise. I can tell from my peripheral vision that the seats behind me are filled to courtroom capacity. My family and members of Germaine's family sat in the seats behind me. There were media reporters and other curious spectators seated behind me as well. I couldn't sense the expressions on their faces because I refused to look behind me for very long. I briefly looked at my mom and sister Joyce to thank them for being there with me. Then the judge walked in, looking around before sitting down. Everyone in the court watched him. I am looking straight ahead at the judge, focused, scared, trying to figure him out. My attorney taps me on my shoulder. "Are you ready Nasihah?" I stare at him without responding. I respond with my eyes. I respond with my beating heart, pounding so hard that I imagined the entire court could feel my nervousness. I have no other choice but to be ready. I couldn't run or hide or not go through with my own trial testimony. A young man was dead and I was being charged with his murder. This was the most critical moment of my life. I was ready to fight for my freedom. I was prepared to tell my side of the story.

The judge speaks: Good morning ladies and gentlemen. Are you ready to precede, Mr. Trachte?

Yes, your Honor.

You may call your first witness, please.

Thank you, your Honor.

Your Honor, the defense calls Nasihah Jones.

In a loud, clear voice, state your name and spell your last name.

Nasihah J-O-N-E-S.

My trial basically came down to me reliving that fatal night. Witnesses were retelling their account of what they remembered from that night. The District Attorney was trying to establish a motive for the shooting outside of me shooting to defend my life and the life of my pregnant girlfriend. All of it was making me feel cornered. It felt like I was being defined and limited to that one night. The fact that I also was a victim of having to endure the painful experience of surviving in the ghetto, including a tragic mistake that caused me to take the life of another youth, was never a factor for the court. No one asked me how I felt standing behind the gun and being the one to pull the trigger. No one asked me whether I felt remorse or not. No one asked me how I felt about losing a child because Germaine had caused Mecca to suffer a miscarriage. All of it haunted me and it still haunts me. No matter how much I try to separate myself from my past and that unfortunate night, bad memories resurface and pursue me. I relive my past because that is what the court requires of me. They want a retelling of that night to determine if I was going to prison or going to be set free.

Although it was six months ago, I still felt very present in that fatal night. My sensations of that night were still fresh; the night sky was still over my head; the rain was still falling; fear and rage still clashed like oil and water, running marathons through my veins. The trial was going to be painful and I was going to be questioned and scrutinized and a conclusion was going to be reached by the jury. Either they will accept my truth of what happened or believe a different inaccurate version.

All I really cared about was the truth coming out. I didn't expect the jury to know my whole life story. I just wanted them to feel my pain. I wanted them to try to walk with me on that night. I wanted them to absorb my fear and imagine themselves in my shoes. I wanted them to be surrounded by the night on a dark city block, the cold rain pounding upon their foreheads and an unknown voice filled with rage yelling at them from the shadows of an alley. I wanted them to know what it felt like to have an angry Black man racing toward them and bent on killing them. I wanted them to ask themselves what they would have done if a crazed man had grabbed their pregnant girlfriend and slammed her to the ground and then reached for what could have been a weapon he might be carrying. Those white jurors did not hold final power over my life. They weren't God. But they were holders of the key to my prison cell. My freedom was on trial so I wanted the truth of that night to be told to the jury. Freedom or jail, I just wanted my story to be heard.

CHAPTER 32

TRIAL RECESS

MY TRIAL reached its first recess. The jurors were escorted to the jury deliberation room and I was taken back to an empty holding cell where I would be served the same old disgusting lunch of a small carton of milk and a bologna sandwich. I wasn't eating meat at the time so I adjusted to eating the outer edges of the bread and drinking the milk just to sustain myself until I got back to jail. The recesses would last anywhere from 30 minutes to an hour. All I could do in that cell was to pace back and forth or just sit on the steel bench and think back about more positive moments of my life. I thought about the time when I actually had hope for better days in my neighborhood. I thought about the time when my brothers and I were actually innocent of and protected from the insanity and misery of our ghetto streets, a time when we knew only peace and love and fun and exploring nature in our backyard, or when we would take walks to a nearby park or to the Hudson River looking for any living thing that wasn't living in our apartment. There was actually a moment when my mother was doing everything she could to save me and my brothers from being exposed to the negative world of our streets. Having very few resources to do so made it almost impossible, but I remember mother often taking us north of the city to the country in Marlboro where many of her Jamaican friends lived and worked as apple pickers or farmers. We always ate exotic foods on the farm, which was the best part of going there. There was so much open land and so many apple trees that my brothers and I would play games like tag, or hide and go seek, or dodge ball with rotten apples.

I thought about the time when I first met Margaret and how she immediately took a liking to me. She believed in me in ways that a mother would believe in her own child. To her, I had so much potential and what she called raw talent. I was but eight years old at the time of our meeting and so full of life and curiosity. I was hungry for knowledge and just loved to doodle or sketch things around me whenever I wasn't running around playing. I thought about the brighter days of my childhood, the days when everything good was open to me, when I was able to dream, to freely dream of becoming whatever I wanted to be: a scientist, a conservationist, a great artist, a doctor.

As a child, in my earlier years, I lived and dreamed in the magic of my imagination. The world then was boundless and I felt powerful, creative, and connected to things outside myself. I had neither experience nor a vocabulary of evil, negativity, or breaking the law. I had no fear of anything. The world was all mine. I was innocent and the world around me was free from the ghetto darkness that consumes and destroys. The sun, the moon, night and day, the worm, the bird, everything that my young mind could imagine existing in this world in my pure innocence I sensed and was part of. It was a harmonious coexistence based on my own curiosity and exploring the world around me.

I thought of those happier childhood days to prevent myself from crying in this holding cell, where I found myself alone with the reality that I was far from that innocent kid who once existed. At one time I thought of myself as a young nature explorer examining life through the small critters in my backyard. Now, not only do I know about death; I am also responsible for the death of another human being. I felt doomed again and even though I found that reminiscing was not comforting me very much during my first trial recess, I continued to think about the happier days of my early childhood.

CHAPTER 33

FLASHBACK

I REMEMBERED my experience at Camp Robins with my two brothers. Camp Robins became our very first summer experience together not far outside Newburgh. Every morning, mother would wake us up about six in the morning to prepare us for our day of fun and activities at the Camp. Every morning became a repetitious ritual that my brothers and I would follow at our mother's command. She was the big chief and we were the little Indians following her orders: 1. Take a bath, 2. Get dressed, 3. Clean your room, 4. Make sure you take care of each other. Mother would make sure that we had our breakfast as well as prepare us a small lunch of turkey and bologna sandwiches, an apple or orange and one fruit juice. She made sure that our back packs were filled with the appropriate items: swimming trunks, underwear and socks, a towel, and a paper listing all of our names, address, mother's name, and emergency contact numbers. Once everything was prepared and we were ready to go off, my two brothers and I would walk to the YMCA on Liberty Street where the bus would pick us up around eight o'clock.

On the camp bus is where the fun began. The bus was filled with a rainbow of children— Blacks, Whites, Latinos, and a few Asian and Native American kids. We were all the same in our eyes. Nothing other than the differing shades of skin separated us. Never did our myriad of colors get in the way of us having fun together. Our differences, the very few that were distinguishable, actually made us more attractive to one another.

From the moment we got on the bus until the moment we reached the camp, we sang songs: Short songs, long songs, old American songs, and patriotic songs. We sang songs that were camp related and songs that were about boats, the forest, animals, and having fun. Having fun was all that mattered. This was a most joyous time of my life and it felt good being a kid and safe. It felt good feeling American and patriotic. There was nothing that could have convinced me that I wasn't equal to the whitest of white kids riding along in the bus with me. Race and racism was not something that parents or teachers talked about with kids. That topic was certainly not necessary at our camp.

When we finally reached the camp, all the children on our bus converged with the larger group of kids who had arrived before us. We all would be divided into groups based on our age and the camp's counselors would outline our daily schedule.

Our activities consisted of playing games, playing more games, learning how to swim, hiking through the woods, observing nature, learning the names of the various animals and insects we spotted, and competing with other teams. That's what Camp Robins was all about and I loved every second of it.

At noon, all the teams would gather back at the dining area for lunch and to be counted to make sure that none of the kids was missing. After lunch, all the children joined with their teams and the rest of the day's activities went on. Our day would end at 2:30. By this time we would usually be exhausted from all of the fun and games and ready to head home to our parents. We would gather for the last time at the dining area, be counted, and called by name to board the bus that would take us back to our neighborhoods. When all of the kids were finally on the bus, there was no more singing songs on the way home. Most of us were drained by all our activities at camp and now could only take a nap while the bus drove us home. Although the day was now coming to an end, we were all happy. We were happy to have had fun, happy to have explored a new world outside the ghetto that we eventually had to go back home to, happy to have been temporarily removed from a negative world that was fast approaching us all.

CHAPTER 34

PETS AT HOME

WE LOVED animals, my brothers and I. When we moved to our new home on First Street, we immediately noticed that our backyard was home to a host of critters. There were garden snakes, all kinds of bugs that we had never seen before, frogs, squirrels, and birds of different colors. These critters probably enjoyed our backyard as much as we did since our yard was the only yard in the neighborhood to have a vegetable garden, an array of plants, and several types of fruit trees. We were fortunate to have a backyard like that when many kids in my neighborhood had nothing at all. And even though our home was surrounded by all of these animals and my mother knew of our affinity to these animals, she had made it clear to us that none of these critters were allowed to enter the house. Of course my brothers and I had different plans.

We began with small critters; ones that we could easily hide from the detective radar of our mother. We made little makeshift homes for spiders, beetles, snails, and Lamyrids out of glass and plastic containers. The more experienced we got with making better habitats for these critters and the better we got at keeping them from mother, the greater the chances we took at bringing bigger animals into the house. For a long time mother never knew that we had small animals and insects living in our bedroom.

One day when my two brothers and I were at a fishing trip on the Hudson River, we came across a small turtle about the size of a half dollar coin. We had never had a turtle as a pet before and really didn't know what turtles ate to survive, but we made it our new pet anyway.

My brother Chris and I constructed an 8" x 11" container using glue and Plexiglas while my brother Marcus was in charge of collecting the grass, rocks, twigs, and anything else that would make our new pet feel at home. Once the turtle's new home was put together, we hid it in our bedroom closet and gave it hours of our attention after school. We would observe the turtle slowly pace back and forth, stretch its neck outward from its small shell and look around before bringing its neck back into its shell. But most of the time the turtle would just sit in the same spot for hours.

After about a week of having the turtle as a pet, we realized that all of the fun of having a pet turtle had dissipated. And even worse, the turtle had stopped eating. We gave it everything that we imagined turtles would eat: lettuce, bread, dead flies, and rice. Nothing seemed to satisfy our pet turtle. We guessed that maybe it didn't eat lettuce and bread, dead flies, and rice. Maybe turtles ate something that our childish imagination could not provide. Or maybe the turtle became sick, homesick after we had taken it from its natural environment and made it a new home inside a closet in a Plexiglas cube with lifeless grass and twigs.

The following morning the three of us agreed that we could no longer take care of the turtle and that it was best that we turn it loose in our backyard among the other creatures that freely enjoyed their home there. After school we were planning to release the turtle but when we returned home we discovered that our turtle was no longer moving. It was as lifeless as the dried brown grass that it lay upon. Our turtle was dead and we all felt guilty for having tried to make it a pet. That was a sad day for my brothers and me. None of us cried but we did feel terribly bad. We tried everything possible to take good care of the turtle but the turtle just wouldn't eat. After dinner we went out back, dug a hole for the little turtle, and had a very childish memorial for the turtle where I acted as a preacher and made my brothers bow their heads as I said a prayer for the turtle. Then we buried it. I wish I could remember exactly what that prayer was but I don't. I just remember us laughing hysterically at me pretending to be a preacher and giving a sermon over our dead pet turtle. That was our last turtle. In fact, we never attempted to make indoor pets out of turtles, frogs, snakes or bugs again.

Later that year my brothers and I tried our luck with dogs. We figured that dogs were manageable and more companion like as opposed to the slow moving and boring turtle we had only a few months earlier— so we thought. In our childhood naivety, we thought that we could bring a stray dog into our house off the streets and train it with no trouble. We ended up changing dogs at least once every two weeks. We had all types of dogs of different breeds and sizes. We tried our luck with large dogs, then miniature dogs, a few old dogs, then some puppies. We had our share of pit bulls and German shepherds and all sorts of mutts. They all seemed to bark when they weren't supposed to, urinated and defecated where they weren't supposed to, smelled when they weren't supposed to, and they were all found by my mother who stuck by her no pets allowed rule. Mother would kick every last dog of ours out of our home, all the same. Looking back, those days were funny and full of excitement; days when my brothers and I would let our curiosity run wild and every day was an adventure. We actually never stopped loving animals despite my mother's reluctance for us to have them. We eventually did get a pet dog that my mother was not against us having in the home, but it would be years later.

CHAPTER 35

THE TRIAL RESUMES

THE SOUND of keys taping against the gate of the holding cell. It is the Court Officer awaking me from my nostalgic daydreams of childhood. He calls out my last name: "Jones! Hey Jones, wake up! They are ready for you!" The gate opens and I am escorted back into the already filled courtroom. My attorney immediately advises me that I will be continuing my testimony, which means that I will have to get back on the witness stand. Once I sit down, facing the courtroom, the Judge begins to speak about an objection that was made before recess.

"The objection that has been made on the last question that was before this witness is overruled. You may proceed."

"I have been the victim of several robberies."

"When was that, Mr. Jones?"

"The last one was at the end of March."

"Could you tell us the circumstances under which that occurred? Describe the incident."

My attorney wanted me to tell the Court what it was like to be a young Black male living in the ghetto. He figured that this all-white jury would need to hear the reality of my experiences if they were ever to be able to empathize with me for carrying a gun for protection. So I begin to candidly speak of every moment when a gun or knife was pointed at me. I look at each and every member of the jury and explain to him or her every moment when I was forced at gunpoint to give up what little money I had. I illustrate to them the reality of hate in the streets, how hate translates into people attacking you for what you have and how everyday becomes a condemnation to a life of fear in your own neighborhood. I attempt to describe in detail what I experienced, where it had occurred, and how I felt afterwards. I try to explain to the white eyes staring at me and listening to me that after every robbery I felt violated and demoralized. These robberies had not been random. I was a target in the streets for what I had. That was just the way it was out there – having material possessions others wanted made you a target. And the fact that I was young and didn't have any older brothers protecting me made me an easy target. Being victimized time after time made me want to get a gun to defend myself. I wanted the jurors to know what it felt like to be victimized, to feel totally powerless to defend yourself. I wanted them to feel my pain and for them to walk in my shoes and understand why I became tired of not being able to defend myself. It was painful having to recall all of these experiences to the jurors, and even more painful to know that these negative encounters in the streets led me to this courtroom, this murder trial.

"How old were you when you first got robbed and did the individuals who robbed you use a weapon?" "I was maybe 12 or 13 years old and yes they did use a weapon to rob me!"

Did you report that incident to the police, Nasihah?"

"Yes."

"And as a result of reporting that to the police, did those individuals, are you aware of whether they became arrested?"

"Yes."

"As a result of that case, did you have any further problems?"

"Yes."

"Can you tell me what those were?"

"The family and friends of the men who robbed me harassed me and continually threatened me because I got the cops involved."

My attorney asks more questions about other robberies I suffered. I tell him and the Court about every last one of them. He asks me why I hadn't reported the latter robberies. I respond that after the first incident I had a lot of problems from the guys who robbed me and from their friends, and I believed that if I reported any of the later robberies to the cops, more bad things would happen to me.

"Nasihah, prior to June 17, 1996, had you met an individual you later learned to be named Germaine Fields?"

"Yes."

"And approximately when did that occur in relation to June 17, 1996?"

"About four weeks before."

"And did you actually, were you actually introduced to him as Germaine Fields, or did you come to learn of him by a different name?"

"A different name."

"What was that?"

"G."

"And did Germaine-- had you known Germaine from the community before that?"

"No."

"Did you learn where Germaine had come from?"

"Florida."

"How did you learn that?"

"He told me."

"As a result of the conversations that you had with Germaine Fields, what did you come to learn about Germaine?"

"Germaine Fields told me that he was down with a gang called the Folk. And that while he was in Florida, he beat up police officers."

"Nasihah, with regard to his explaining to you that he had been

down with a gang called the Folk, did he show you anything to substantiate or try and prove that claim?"

"Yes, he showed me several tattoos on his body."

"As a result of his association with that gang, did he tell you about any sort of conduct that he had engaged in or things that he had done with that gang?"

"Your Honor, I would ask that these three photographs be marked as Defendant's Exhibits."

"Nasihah, do these photographs truly and accurately reflect the tattoos that Germaine Fields showed you in the latter parts of May and June of 1996 when you were having conversations regarding his gang association?"

"Yes."

"Your Honor, I would move defendant's photographs into evidence."

"Nasihah, do you see the picture in front of you?"

"Could you describe as best you can that photograph?"

"Well, Germaine Fields told me that it's a pitch fork with the hook hanging off the pitch fork which represents the letter C for the Crips."

"And where did he show you that he had that tattoo on his body?"

"On his back."

My lawyer showed more photos of Germaine's tattoos and I was expected to tell the Court what Germaine told me they represented.

"This tattoo on his arm, it says 'Heat Blunt.' And the 'G' with the hook hanging off of it on his arm he said represented 'Gangster' and 'Crip.' 'Heat' represented a gun. And 'Blunt' meant the thing you smoke marijuana out of."

"And with regard to the word "Heat," he indicated to you that meant a weapon or a gun?"

"A gun."

"And did he indicate to you whether or not in Florida he had-- in this association with the Crips gang -- that he had possessed a gun?"

"Yes."

"Nasihah, when Germaine showed you these tattoos and explained them to you, how did that make you feel?"

"Well I understood that he was trying to intimidate me for whatever reason by showing me his gang tattoos in the first place. So initially it made me feel kind of nervous about him because he was older than me and I heard about the Crips and I knew that it was a dangerous gang. So I felt kind of scared."

"Now Nasihah, following that conversation, did you have-- and prior to June 17, 1996, did you ever have any other occasions to come in contact with Germaine Fields who you knew as "G"?"

"Yes."

"And could you describe that for me?"

"Well, one night I was walking to my girlfriend's house and someone ran out of an alley and grabbed me from behind by placing me in a choke hold. He had a gun pressed against my head and stuck his hand in my pocket taking out my money. Then he turned me around so that I was face to face with him. That person was Germaine. He just laughed at me and said that bad things happen at night and that this was how easy it was to get someone. He laughed, gave me my money back and then just walked off."

"Did you report that incident to the police, Nasihah?"

"No."

"Why not?"

"Because I didn't think at that time that he was really trying to hurt me or rob me since he knew me and gave me my money back. I didn't know what his intentions were actually. And calling the cops was something that I was unwilling to do because of the consequences of snitching to the cops." I understood that the No Snitching Policy of the streets was not just a casual saying; it was a rule that if not respected left you liable to get hurt. So within the context of my real life on the streets, police protection and calling the police after a robbery were nonexistent options.

"Now other than those incidents, did you have any contact with Germaine Fields prior to June 17, 1996?"

"Yes."

"And would you describe that?"

"Well, my girlfriend told me that Germaine was harassing her. So I went to Germaine and asked him whether this was true."

"And why did you do that?"

"Because my girlfriend was pregnant and I was concerned about her and my unborn child."

"And what happened after that conversation?"

"Well, I asked Germaine about the situation but he didn't answer me. He just walked away."

"Now Nasihah, prior to June 17, 1996, did there come a time when you came in possession of a weapon?"

"Yes."

"When was that?"

"A month or two before June 17, 1996."

"And can you tell me why you decided to get a weapon?"

"Because I was... I was in a lot of situations where people used to follow me home, and rob me of my money and jewelry that my sister bought for me."

"Nasihah, do you remember June 17, 1996?"

"Yes."

"What were you doing that day?"

"My girlfriend and I were walking on Lutheran Street."

"When you were with your girlfriend at her house, what were you doing there?"

"I was getting my hair braided."

"And Nasihah, just one thing further. Do you recall an incident when your girlfriend and your sister and you were on the porch prior to June 17, 1996, at your sister's house?"

"Yes."

"And did you have conversations with your girlfriend and your sister regarding Germaine Fields?"

"Yes."

"And did your girlfriend say something to you regarding something that Germaine Fields had said to her?"

"Yes."

"And what was that?"

"Germaine told her that he's going to kill me."

"Now, did she say something further with regard to how, or any other type of statements regarding that?"

"She said that he said that he was going to stab me in my stomach since I was really skinny. He knew how to kill people with knives, and since I was skinny, he's going to stab me in my stomach."

"Now, bringing you back to June 17. You were over at your girlfriend's house on Lutheran Street, correct?"

"Yes."

"And what were you doing there?"

"We were on the porch and she was braiding my hair."

"And how long did that go on for?"

"Around two hours."

"And what did you do after that?"

"We went walking."

"Where did you walk to?"

"We took a walk to the park, around the neighborhood, and back to Lutheran Street."

"And how long were you gone for while you two were walking?"

"Two and a half hours maybe."

"So you got back to Lutheran Street about 9:30 or so?"

"Yeah."

"And what did you do after that?"

"We were just talking about our unborn baby and regular teenager stuff."

"And then around-- drawing your attention to around 11:00 pm, can you tell me what happened?"

"My girlfriend and I, we were walking up Lutheran Street when we heard a voice calling my girlfriend Mecca's name. Because it was really dark on that street we couldn't see anyone and we had not at first recognized the voice yelling in the darkness. But we knew that it was coming from the opposite side of the street. Then all of a sudden, the person who was calling Mecca's name rushed over toward us, and that person was Germaine Fields."

"And what happened when he came over toward you fast?"

"He ran up to me and started yelling and cursing at me."

"And when he was yelling and cursing at you, how close was he to you?"

"Face to face."

"Did he actually come in physical contact with you?"

"He was bumping his chest against mine."

"And when you say he was cursing at you, what was he saying?"

"He was saying, 'What the fuck are you doing here on this block' and for me to get the hell out of there before he kills me. He also said that he wants to hurt me and that I better leave."

"What did you say to him?"

"I asked him, 'What was he talking about? And why was he in my face.' I wanted him to leave me alone. I wanted him not to bother my pregnant girlfriend and me."

"And what happened then?"

"He wasn't listening. He kept yelling and screaming, trying to grab onto me. Then my girlfriend's father ran up the street to where we were."

"When he continued to yell and scream, what types of things was he saying?"

"Get the fuck out of here before you get killed. He was saying things like that. Then my girlfriend's father jumped in."

"How did that make you feel when he was getting in your face and yelling those things at you?"

"Scared."

"What happened after he continued to yell and curse in your face?"

"My girlfriend's father told Germaine to leave us alone."

"And who did he say that to?"

"Germaine."

"And what happened when he said that?"

"Germaine ran up to him, in his face and started yelling at him."

"And what did you do then?"

"I told Germaine to leave him alone, that he was an old man."

"And when you told Germaine to leave your girlfriend's father alone, what happened then?"

"He jumped back into my face."

"And tell us what happened?"

"He was trying to grab onto me. And my girlfriend was pushing Germaine off me. Then my girlfriend's father grabbed me."

"And when he grabbed you, what did you do?"

"My girlfriend's father said, 'Come on Nas, just go down the street!'

"Did he actually grab onto you?"

"Yes."

"And when he said that to you, what did you do?"

"I began to walk along with him with my back---

I was walking backwards, watching Germaine."

"So you walked-- are you saying that you walked backwards with your girlfriend's father, watching Germaine and Mecca?"

"Yes."

"And your girlfriend's father would have been facing toward you at that time hanging on to you while you were facing towards Mecca and Germaine?"

"Yes."

"Now, as you started to back off, could you see what Mecca and Germaine were doing?"

"Yes."

"What was going on?"

"Germaine was grabbing her, throwing her up against a wall."

"What was your girlfriend trying to do?"

"She was trying to get away. She was trying to follow us but Germaine wouldn't let her go."

"And did it appear that your girlfriend was trying to do anything to him in the way of holding him back or pushing him back or what did you see?"

"Yes. Germaine tried to run toward me, but she was pulling him back."

"When you say pulling him back, do you mean in an effort to keep him away from you or go towards you?"

"Away from me."

"And you were backing away, is that correct?"

"Yes."

"And was Mecca, from what you could see, was Mecca able to hold Germaine back?"

"No."

"Tell me what happened? Tell me what happened as you were backing up?"

"Well, my girlfriend was trying to hold Germaine back from getting towards me and they began to struggle, and then we saw Germaine throw Mecca to the ground."

"When you saw Germaine throw Mecca to the ground, what did you do?"

"Well I did what any man would do if you see your pregnant girlfriend being thrown to the ground. Mecca's father let go of me and I ran to her rescue."

"And what happened when you ran up to her?"

"I was trying to pick her up from the ground, but she was unconscious. She had blacked out. She wouldn't get up."

"And what happened when you tried to get your girlfriend up from the ground?"

"Germaine was holding onto her. I was calling Mecca's name, telling her to get up. Germaine wouldn't let go. He wouldn't let go, and he started reaching for something in his pocket. He put his hand inside of his pocket. It looked like he had a gun in his pocket because his pocket was bulging."

"What did you think was in his pocket?"

"A gun."

"What did you do when you saw him reaching for his pocket?"

"Well, he's reaching really quick and still had a hold on Mecca. As soon as he put his hand in his pocket, I pulled out my gun and fired." I didn't think twice. I didn't hesitate. I just fired.

"How did you feel when this was happening?"

"Everything happened so fast. I felt scared."

"What were you scared of?"

"Well, I knew that Germaine carried a gun, and I thought that if I didn't try to stop him, he would have killed Mecca or me."

"Were you thinking at all about Mecca and her condition?"

"Yes."

"How did you feel about that?"

"I was thinking about the baby and thinking about my girlfriend because she was unconscious. I thought she could have hit her head or something because she was not moving."

"When you fired that shot, how many shots went off?"

"Two."

"And this weapon you had was it-- it was an automatic weapon?"

"Yes."

"Now, when the shots went off, what happened?"

"Mecca jumped up and I grabbed her. Then we ran."

"Where did you run to?"

"We ran to my sister's house."

"When you shot Germaine, what were you trying to do?"

"I was aiming at his shoulder. I wasn't trying to kill him. I just wanted to stop him so he wouldn't kill my pregnant girlfriend or me."

"Nothing further, your Honor."

After my attorney finished his examination, his questioning of me, the District Attorney was ready for his cross-examination. The D.A.'s questioning came like rapid fire. It seemed as though he was more concerned with throwing a million questions at me instead of listening to my answers. My story did not change and it wasn't going to. I was the only one there who was fully conscious of everything that had happened. But the District Attorney didn't seem concerned with the truth or at least my version of the truth. He tried to twist everything I said around to have the jurors think that I was somehow lying about what had happened. It was in his best interest to make me the aggressor. He was painting a picture of me as a young gangster with a gun. He described me to the jurors as a thug and a menace who provoked a situation and acted in cold blood. That description of me was farthest from the truth and from the known facts of the case. But someone was dead and I was the shooter so it was convenient and rather easy for the District Attorney to play into the fears of the white jurors — a Black teen with an illegal gun who gunned down a rival gang member. That was his story to the jurors.

One way or another he was going to send me off to prison. He created a false narrative that I was unfit to be free and my future had to be inside a prison cell. To him, and he was trying to persuade the jurors to believe this as well, I was all that was wrong with Newburgh; I was one of the people who brought Newburgh down. Who those people were, he never did say. Part of his narrative was vague and filled with nebulous statements that took away my humanity and made me a monster. At the end of the day it was all about a conviction for the

State of New York. There was no empathy in the courtroom. Not for a Black man anyway. I was nothing more than a black fly trapped in a white web and the District Attorney was the spider sent to kill me and to present my body as a feast to the System. A conviction wasn't justice. It wasn't going to bring Germaine back. It wasn't going to stop the hundreds of thousands of young Black and brown boys from following right behind me into the web of the System. We were all flies destined for the same fate. And the System made no exception for any of us and didn't plan to. The courtroom jargon was already set: view defendants in the worst light, deny their humanity, get a conviction and send them off to the belly of the beast and keep the cycle going. I imagined that there were prisons upstate filled with thousands of Black men and new beds and facilities being made to house a million more.

I was a monster on trial who had no right to protect my own girlfriend and unborn child. Human beings can act in fear and protect their life for survival, but not a Black man. I was a monster because I had acted in self-defense and took the law into my own hands. It didn't matter that everything had happened so fast that night and that I was overtaken by my need to survive and to protect. The District Attorney didn't want to consider my motivations. That of course was not in the best interest of the Court. I remember the District Attorney marching around the courtroom like a juggernaut. I could not defend myself against him and my court-appointed public defender lawyer who was too nonchalant to come to my rescue most of the time.

The DA was too powerful and overwhelming. I was just a kid, still frightened and traumatized by the night of the shooting. Now I felt even more powerless, weak, debased and fragile. His attack on me made me feel like my skull was crushing. My bones were breaking. My spine was being smashed and shattered into a trillion little pieces. My powerlessness made me realize that I was nothing more than a black dot lost in the sea of whiteness surrounding me. I was nothing and the prosecutor was ripping my young life apart. I was already guilty and had a difficult challenge to prove my innocence. All I had was my true story of how I acted only in self-defense to protect the life of my unborn child, my girlfriend and myself.

The Court called a recess until the following morning. I was escorted back to my cell and told by my attorney to get some rest. I was emotionally and psychologically drained from my day in court. When I got back to my cell I went right to the faucet, turned the water on and threw cold water on my face. It was refreshing to the surface of my face but it did nothing for my soul. The core of my being— heart, lungs, brain, and eyes felt like they were on fire. I couldn't see the future of my life, how all of this would one day turn out. My freedom was already gone. I'd been in confinement awaiting trial for the past six months. My situation wasn't looking hopeful. It was getting darker by the day. The white eyes of the court refused to understand what it was like to live life in the streets. They often look at the ghetto as a jungle but then deny the context and condition in which Black humans must survive. My going from the jungle to a cage confirmed all of their racist ideas of the Black male being an animal. The pressure on me was overwhelming. The walls were closing in on me and my cell was spinning in violent circles. The steel bed, the dirty faucet, the metal toilet, the graffiti and toothpaste plastered on the cell's concrete walls were crushing me. I didn't want to spend the rest of my life behind these walls. The thought of my young life coming to a close made me extremely depressed. I ended my very bad day in court drifting off to sleep.

Summations were to begin the next day. Both attorneys were going to put on a theatrical show before the jurors to convince them of my innocence or my guilt. Summations were the defense and prosecution interpretation and retelling of selected events. Jurors were expected not to take these accounts at face value. But there was no way of determining how influenced jurors actually were by these summations. I personally learned a great lesson about how trials are won and lost.

The facts of the case, what really happened, the subjective standard and the objective standard mean absolutely nothing, or very little in the end. Jurors are not legal experts or lawyers themselves. They are selected layman expected to be temporary unbiased interpreters of the law. So in the end what really matters is who can articulate the best version of facts and ultimately persuade jurors that their version is the truth. Facts and evidence do not stand on their own. Selected facts become persuasive instruments used to make or break an argument. Facts are twisted and that seems to be the American way of justice. Empirical evidence is thrown out the window. Who can tell the better story? Who can paint the best picture? Who can convince the jurors? This is the reason why high priced attorneys will always be more effective than Court appointed attorneys. This is the reason why the poor are almost always convicted despite their innocence or guilt and the reason why the rich are less likely to be convicted than poor defendants.

Many trials come down to which side has a bigger bank account. He who buys the best attorney and better expert witnesses to construct a persuasive story wins. Money buys facts, witness accounts, testimonies, outright lies, perjury, and control over a case. The facts sometimes don't matter. It comes down to who can bend the facts more skillfully to fit the desired result of a guilty verdict or an acquittal. I'm not in the position to make a condemnation of the entire American judicial system but I know that the way my own trial was conducted was no more than a verbal boxing match where truth and fact were slain and replaced by the ignorant theories of people who would never step foot in the ghetto of Newburgh.

I sat quietly through both attorneys' arguments to the jurors. The stares from all those eyes directed at me along with the coldness of the courtroom had me shivering as if I was actually standing outside in the dead of winter. The flesh on my back was stinging because the District Attorney's choice of words to describe me felt like a sharp machete slashing jagged cuts into me. I was nothing more than a Black animal finally captured and deserving to be quickly thrown into a cage. Part of me wished that the jurors would somehow ignore the negative and false epithets used by the District Attorney. But another part of me realized that the D.A. was playing into the deep subconscious fears of the white jurors: A Black kid from the ghetto carrying a gun, a loaded gun, ready to shoot and perhaps kill. Forget his young age and gentle demeanor. He is a vigilante, taking the law into his own hands, his own hands, killing another youth. What an outrage. What an erosion of the values of our society. First a Black kid kills, what's next? If not put away forever, he will one day harm you! The DA was not that blatant in his oration but that is what he meant and the jurors knew it. His critique of me wasn't about me. It was more about what I represented to society; society being the all-white jurors. His performance was so apocalyptic and alarming that my attorney was forced to remind the jurors to separate the O.J. Simpson case that happened a few years earlier from my case. My case was nowhere as huge as the Simpson case but where Simpson was found not guilty against the beliefs of a white audience, my case could become that same white audience's vengeance.

The fact of the matter is, I realize now as I had realized then, that race is the burden of those whom the System was not intended to protect from the beginning. Kids in possession of firearms are a grave detriment to our society, period. Race exacerbates this crisis because of not only white fears that still linger on from the white guilt of slavery and white fear of slave vengeance unfulfilled, but also the fact that the great majority of victims of Black kids with firearms will in fact be other Black kids. The justifications for why we ghetto Blacks feel we need guns never escapes the confines of our own world. We lack the necessary education to understand our own oppression, and our own power to define a new way to confront this oppression, with the opposite of violence, with love and compassion and a re-definition of our humanity.

Instead we add to the quiet and slow genocide of our own race, we internalize over and over again a suppressed pain, and without warning or the slightest form of disrespect, we willfully spit this pain into the face of the Blacks around us. This was something that I figured was not in the mind of the District Attorney. Not then and perhaps not ever. But I was thinking. I was imagining. A conviction would satisfy the Court but it will not bring back Germaine and it will certainly never represent justice in the way that justice should be rendered. After this case comes to a close, another set of defendants and victims will take this stage—both youth; both Black; both already victims of a society that had already determined them losers before they were born.

CHAPTER 36

SUMMATIONS

"GOOD MORNING, ladies and gentlemen. You sat through a trial where you have heard a number of people witness a very tragic, quick event. You are going to be asked how to consider and analyze the facts as you heard them apply to the law as Judge Patsalos will inform you the law exists. You will be asked to consider a number of counts regarding homicide. I ask you to consider when analyzing whether or not this 15 year old, and everything that he did, whether his conscious aim or objective, whether it was his intent to kill Germaine Fields. When he came running across the street at him, did he pull a gun at him? Did he want to pull that gun? Was he willing to back away, or did he react to a situation when he saw his girlfriend, very close girlfriend, young love? I understand they're 15 and 16. It was a very serious relationship. She's pregnant with his child. He witnesses her hit the ground with Germaine Fields. He rushes up. He sees what he has to deal with. He deals with it, and it happens in a couple of seconds. And he does what he does. . ."

"You are going to consider Nasihah's testimony. You are going to consider what type of kid he was. How old he was. You are going to consider whether at 15 you conceptualize the severity of the things that you are doing in a certain situation, whether you conceptualize life or death situations, whether he was trying to injure Germaine Fields so he could get his girlfriend and himself away safely, or whether he actually was acting with such a depraved mind or an intentional mind that he intended to kill him...."

"You heard his testimony, you saw the young man. You heard from his family. You heard about his family upbringing. He's not an intentional killer. He told you. The case is not about who shot the gun because he came in and told you 'I shot the gun. I felt I had to shoot the gun.' His intent was not to murder Germaine Fields. This was not depravity to the extent that it wasn't reasonable. . ."

"The last homicide crime you are going to be asked to consider is Manslaughter in the Second Degree, whether there was conscious, reckless disregard of the risk. This is a lesser standard than that which is required for murder under depraved indifference. . ."

"He was a young man who was fearful. He was a young man growing up in a community where he had access to weapons; he was able to buy the pistol for a few bucks on the street. Is that okay? That is terrible. That is wrong.... Possessing that weapon is a crime for which Nasihah will have to be punished because he did not have a license for that weapon. He did not have that weapon in his home or place of business. . ."

"He understands he's going to be punished for carrying a weapon. It's wrong. We cannot have 15-year-old kids carrying loaded semiautomatic weapons in their pockets. It cannot be allowed by our society, but that is not where the case begins. He had the weapon in his pocket, and he came into the situation that he came into. He didn't carry that weapon with intent to use it against another person. He carried the weapon because he thought it would be the right thing to do to protect himself.

"Consider what he knew. You heard a lot of witnesses in the case. Some of them saw it from far away. It was dark. They couldn't see the faces. It's 11:00 at night. There's dim streetlight.... No one is lying in the case. It's what we talked about in the jury selection. It's perception.

What they saw, where they saw it. How much time they had to observe what they had to observe...."

"The interesting part about how intense this dispute on the street was is that Larry Jackson from the second floor of his apartment watching cartoons hears these voices so intense, yelling and screaming, threatening, that it brings him downstairs to watch on the porch.... Think about whether you have ever been involved in a confrontation, even just a minor one with someone you love, when you get really upset and you are yelling at them and they're yelling back at you and how nervous and intense that makes you feel and how much you sometimes do things that you just don't think about or say things that you just don't think about. You just don't intend to do it."

"The two young lovers were there every day, every single day together for a year and a half. Nasihah had gone over to Mecca's house. He had his hair braided at 5:00, having a good time, they went for a walk in the park, and did whatever they do. Probably were concerned about the fact that she's 16 and he's 15. And she is pregnant, but they're doing the best they can. They're getting along. They're trying to have a good time out on the streets that night...."

"And here comes Germaine Fields. He rushes across the street so aggressively that Mecca's father who says and I believe him, that 'I don't interfere in Mecca's business. She's 16; you try and give your 16-year-old some latitude.' But this obviously makes him afraid. And he comes over. He tries to intercept. When Germaine comes over, he gets face to face with Nasihah."

"You know how frightening that is to have somebody yelling in your face? And I'm sorry that I had to have Nasihah testify to what he said. No one wants to hear that language, but Germaine is face to face with him, saying to him, 'What the fuck are you doing with Mecca. Get out of here. I'll kill you.' And that's how he was saying it because it brought people out from down the block. And an adult tried to enter into the situation and say, 'Hey, Germaine, easy, you know. Go, you know, this is a boyfriend and girlfriend. You are not involved in this situation. Get back across the street. What are you doing?"

"And what does Germaine do? Did he say okay, Mr. Smith, no problem? He turned around and jumped on him, yelling and screaming the same way... Now, Mecca's father is an experienced guy out on the street too, apparently, and he said he wasn't afraid. But he was afraid because he didn't take Germaine and get him out of the situation because he couldn't. He did what he could. He grabbed Nasihah because Germaine was too aggressive. Germaine was in his face yelling and screaming and then backed off of him because he was after Nasihah. 'What the fuck are you doing with her?' Germaine yelled. And Nasihah responded, 'Hey, this is my girlfriend. What do you mean? What are you talking about? I'm here minding my business with my girlfriend.'"

"He's got to be thinking, why? What is this guy doing? Mecca's father grabs Nasihah. He's doing his best to try to diffuse the situation. And Nasihah, no doubt scared and probably happy to have his girlfriend's father grab him, backs up. He's backing away from the situation. Does he want to use that gun in his pocket? Obviously he does not. Because when he was face to face with Germaine, scared out of his mind, he could have taken it out right there and shot him. He didn't want to use that weapon. He's scared out of his mind. He wants it to be over. So he's backing away faced toward Germaine because he's watching his pregnant girlfriend and is afraid for her."

"Germaine was grabbing at her, pushing her, pushing her back, always getting closer and closer to Nasihah. And then what happened? They went down to the ground. Everyone said they had seen bodies fall to the ground. And when they fell, they fell hard. And they fell on cement. So much so that it blacked Mecca out for a few seconds.

And Nasihah ran to the aid of his girlfriend. He was not only concerned for her, he was concerned for their child. I know they're 16 and 15. They shouldn't be having a baby. But they were. Put yourself in their situation. Say it's your loved one that you know is pregnant. You see her get slammed to the ground. And whom did she slam on the ground with? This guy you barely knew, but what did you know about him the first time you met him when he just moved up from Florida? He got arrested for assaulting a police officer. That's what he told Nasihah. He was a Crip gang member. That takes a pretty seriously violent individual."

"But it's not okay to break the law. He had the gun. You can't have the gun. He's got to be punished for that... The Judge is going to instruct you that after you consider the four different levels of homicide, and I submit to you that if you consider them honestly and truthfully, that there is no way that you can consider that this 15-year-old kid did what he did with the intent to murder somebody or that his conduct was so depraved. This isn't a guy who is shooting everybody out into the crowd and expecting to kill somebody or running down the sidewalk. It's not murder. It's not depraved indifference."

"I ask that you put the burden on the People, as the Judge will instruct you, to prove beyond a reasonable doubt that he was not acting in self-defense or defense of another. You may use deadly physical force when you reasonably believe that such force, such use of deadly physical force, is necessary to defend yourself or a third person from what you reasonably believe to be the imminent use of deadly physical force against yourself or a third person."

"Verbal quarrels are not enough. But if you reasonably believe that another person is about to use deadly physical force upon you or upon another, you don't have to wait to get shot. You don't have to wait to have him pounding your girlfriend's head into the cement worse than he already did. You don't have to wait if your own mind is operating as a reasonable person would, you can use deadly physical force... God, I pray for us all that we're never ever put in that situation. But Nasihah was, and judge him as if you were in his shoes."

"Nasihah thought Germaine had pushed it to the level that he was going to pull a weapon out on him. Germaine had his girlfriend. Nasihah couldn't get his girlfriend up. He saw Germaine doing what he was doing. He was going for his pocket, and Nasihah had to decide right then and there. He didn't have as long as all the testimony took during the trial. He certainly didn't have as long as I'm taking to explain it to you. He had a second. He had a split second, and he had a gun. And he had to decide what to do. He knew he couldn't take this guy. He knew if Germaine pulled a knife, he might get stabbed or his girlfriend would. He knew that if Germaine had pulled out a gun, he might shoot him or his girlfriend. He had to decide right then and there what to do."

"He reasonably believed, he believed in his mind that he or his girlfriend were going to get killed or so seriously physically injured that they were going to lose the baby, or they were going to be damaged by what they experienced. She blacked out. She was not responding. He thought she was already seriously physically injured, for God sake. What do you and I do in this situation? He had a gun. He tries to back away. He's confronted. It's intense. The guy is in his face. He thinks the guy is dangerous and violent. He slams his girlfriend down onto the cement. She blacks out. She wasn't responding. Germane bent over. Nasihah thought he was going for a weapon. He took out his weapon first. He shot him. And he shot twice. And he ran."

"He didn't know whether he had hurt him or whether he killed him. He didn't know. He was frightened. He ran. Mecca jumped up and they were finally able to get away. He was finally able to get away from that very bad situation. He had to get away because he tried everything else. It's hard to believe, but it took that gunshot to get away. Because Germaine would not let go. He was acting as he appeared to Mecca's father and to Nasihah, as if he was high on drugs. And he was acting crazy. He wasn't making any sense. He wouldn't stop."

"Ladies and gentlemen, Nasihah Jones was a 15-year-old kid on the street. An older male that was a Crips gang member was intimidating him. He was attacked verbally. He tried to back away, and his girlfriend was attacked physically."

"Ladies and gentlemen, Nasihah Jones comes from a nice family. He's a school kid. He's an artist. He is not a murderer, ladies and gentlemen. He sits here, he told you the story. He doesn't look like a murderer. He doesn't act like a murderer. You know why? He's not a murderer. He didn't want to do it that night. But he did it. He's going to have to be punished for possessing the gun illegally because we can't let him possess the gun. But, he did. I submit to you, ladies and gentlemen, that if a stranger came across the street at you, attacked your loved one when she was pregnant, fell onto the ground with her, and wouldn't let her go, and you had a gun in your pocket, and you thought he was going for a weapon in his pocket, you would shoot him. He did that. But it's not murder. The law does not define it as a murder because the law allows you to protect yourself, and it allows you to protect those you love."

"And you can render the right verdict. The right verdict is that he is not guilty of anything but possessing the loaded weapon without a permit."

My defense attorney and the prosecutor were now finished arguing their cases before the jurors. I sat there, quiet, anxious, nervous, not knowing what the outcome would be, not knowing in what direction my life would turn next. My fate was entirely in the hands of 12 jurors whom I knew nothing about, 12 jurors who were given two interpretations of who I am. On one hand, a decent kid from the streets of Newburgh who had it terribly rough growing up in a negative environment. And on the other hand, I was just another bastard child already criminalized and ghettoized into the life of gangs, guns, and ghetto mischief. I thought about which interpretation of me the jurors would believe. What was more fathomable and digestible to them? What image related more to what they already believed, what they already knew, what they have already been exposed to? Could I really be a decent kid who just had it rough in Newburgh? A "*school kid*" my attorney called me, but would they believe that about me? An artist I was. But would that excuse the fact that I was being charged for murder? Could I really have been so frightened by the negative and threatening life around me that it drove me to purchase an illegal gun in order to protect myself? Did I really believe that Germaine was going to hurt my pregnant girlfriend? Did I really believe that Germaine had a weapon on him that night?

After some time had gone by, the Judge began to charge the jurors with his instructions on the law. This went on for at least an hour with the Judge informing them of what they could do and what they could not do, and what they were to accept and what they were not to accept. What each charge meant and how they were to view each charge.

The more the Judge talked about instructions and rules and procedures, the more I became confused. Everything was so technical and became a blur— the jargon, the procedures, the instructions, the process, the setting, all of it. Everything was overwhelming and energy consuming. I felt aloof, far removed from the whole experience since the beginning because most of the legal language was foreign to me and never explained. And now things were coming to a close. Just like that, it would come down to twelve jurors deciding what should happen to me.

The Judge speaks: "In order to reach a verdict, all 12 members of the jury must agree. Your verdict must be unanimous. Whenever all of you are in agreement on a verdict, you may report your verdict to the Court."

The Judge talked some more to the Jurors about their duty in the case, and after about 30 minutes of talking, the Judge retired the jury into the jury room to begin their deliberations.

CHAPTER 37

THE VERDICT

MOMENTS LATER, I recall the jurors sending a note out to the Court requesting that they be given a written copy of the charges. The jurors were called back into the Courtroom. The Judge responded by saying that he was unable to comply with their request but that he could read back any charges to them. They retire again. Another note. They enter the Courtroom. The Judge speaks. This time he says that it is his understanding that Tylenol is on its way. Then he reads the Jurors note: *"We the Jury request the following: one, to be read back to the Jury, murder in the second degree, depraved indifference, manslaughter in the first degree, intentional manslaughter in the second degree, reckless."* The Judge reads the charges back to the Jury. They retire. Another note. They re-enter the Courtroom. The Judge speaks. *"We require a better explanation of depraved indifference. We require murder in the second degree, depraved indifference be read again.*

"At this point, there may not be any better explanation that I can give you regarding depraved indifference than what I have already read," the Judge says.

The jury retires. Another note. They re-enter the Court. The Judge speaks. "I will read depraved indifference murder again to the Jury as requested." The jurors retire again. The Judge speaks later. *"It's 7:00.*

It seems to me that the Jury has been busy for quite some period of time and unless either Counsel has any comments they wish to make, it's the Court's intention to sequester the Jury at this time and let them get a good night's rest and get back tomorrow and continue with their deliberations."

The next day it was the same routine. The Jurors retired. A note comes out with a request. The Jurors enter the Courtroom. The Judge speaks. "We the Jury request the following: The instructions to be read back as pertaining to the charges." The Judge reads the instructions. The jury retires.

Another note. "We need read to us by the Court stenographer what the Judge said to us after closing arguments and before the instructions that you just read to us." The judge reads to the jury what they requested. They retire once more.

Another note. We need murder in the second degree, depraved indifference, and also manslaughter in the second degree, intentional, read to us. The judge speaks. *"Under our law, a person is guilty of murder in the second degree when under circumstances evincing a depraved indifference to human life, he or she recklessly engages in conduct which creates a grave risk of death to another person, and thereby causes the death of that person. Manslaughter, in the first degree, under the law a person is guilty of manslaughter in the first degree when with intent to cause serious physical injury to another person he or she causes the death of such person."* The jury retires.

Another note. The Judge speaks. *"The last note that we have received indicates that the Jury has reached a verdict. I will bring in the jury."*

The jury enters the Court. The Judge speaks. *"Ladies and gentlemen, I have your last note. It says, we, the jury have come to a verdict."*

My heart was beating faster and harder. Knees buckling under me, I felt faint in the anticipation of what was to come next. I wanted to believe that there was no way that the jurors could find me guilty of murder when it was obvious that I had no intent of killing Germaine and apparent that I was not the aggressor. If anything they would empathize with me and put themselves in my shoes. They would see that I had acted in self-defense, just as they would if they found themselves in a similar crisis. But I would soon learn a hard lesson about people when it comes to making sense of matters involving others that do not fit their understanding of defending their right to live. The beating of my heart transcended my own body and the four walls of that courtroom. My heart was the African drum, the war drum, warning my tribe that foreign invaders were here to do us no good. They were going to capture us, break us, destroy our humanity in a way that we could never fully be restored – even if freedom was one day achieved by us.

"Mr. Foreperson, would you please rise," the Judge says in the direction of the jurors. This was the climax of my trial. That final moment when my case will be settled one way or another. I can hear my heart beating louder and louder. "Would the defendant please rise," the Judge says. I stand. The jurors stare at me. I stare back. My eyes were darting side to side, questioning their unknown thoughts. The suspense was surreal and nothing could calm my heart from wanting to tear through my chest. The Foreperson seemed to be moving in slow motion, his gesture of standing and facing the Court seemed disconnected. He was facing me. His words would be directed at me. Only I could hear the hidden truth behind what was really being said. We stare at each other in a moment that we will never see again – a white man and a Black boy dangling on a thin rope of time, wrestling against history for justice, both trying to settle our search for a greater humanity. With my condemnation perhaps he will feel safer, more free from unfettered Black rage running through the streets of America. My death is his salvation. On the other hand, white affirmation of Black life is what mattered to me. Only he could humanize me and set the record straight that I too was a human being with the right to defend my life. A Black world was unimaginable where whites did not have to settle our fate. From the moment I left my mother's womb, I was bombarded with white myths and the ethos of a white god, white angels, white heroes and explorers and colonizers. I grew up with white cops terrorizing my neighborhood with their white presence and power. Now at 15, after a grave conflict with my own kind, my own kin, another brother, I am one black fly caught in the eye of the web and all around me are the same white faces I have seen all my life, waiting to either validate or condemn me forever.

I needed the jurors to walk in my shoes on that night. I was expecting them to understand how the fear and rage and pain had ripped through the night air, leaving behind emotional and mental scars that would be visible for the rest of our lives. Everyone became a victim that night — Germaine, Mecca, her father, our community, and me. That conflict made rationality cease and reason die. Black bodies pitted against one another stifled intelligent action and arrested the divine within us. It was more than a conflict. It was war and my world was spinning out of control. Darkness reigned over the hoods that we passionately called home. The screaming savage words, "I'm going to kill you!" "What the fuck are you doing here?" "Get the fuck out of here before I murder you!" all echo through the night. I expected the jurors to hear those words. I expected Germaine's words to paint a picture of how dreadful that night was for me. I wanted them to see the silhouette of struggling bodies grappling on that dark street. I wanted them to see a pregnant Mecca smacking onto the concrete stomach first. I wanted them to know what it felt like when your world stops spinning.

You hear nothing.

You see nothing.

Then you are suddenly awakened by the clapping sound of gunshots. I am still standing and Germaine is slumped on the concrete somewhere in the darkness. I can't see him but I know he is there. I never had the chance to ask him what drove him to such rage that he wanted to threaten my life, and I never will get that chance. Perhaps the 12 jurors held that answer along with my fate.

"Has the Jury agreed upon a verdict?" says the Judge.

"Yes, we have," replied the Foreman of the jurors.

"How say you as to count one charging the defendant with murder in the second degree, intentional murder, guilty or not guilty?"

"Not guilty!" the Foreperson states.

"How say you as to count two charging the defendant with murder in the second degree, depraved indifference, guilty or not guilty?"

"Guilty!"

I died right there in the courtroom. I felt I was dreaming, and if I was not dreaming then I did not want to live with that guilty verdict cast against me. I remember my legs giving out and the seat behind me catching my fall. My attorney standing beside me hammered his fists into the table yelling at the jurors, "Bullshit! Bullshit!" He cried out, "No way, fuck no! My client is no murderer!" He wondered as I wondered how the jurors came to that decision. The jurors obviously arranged the evidence of my case in a different way than my attorney had laid it out.

My mother and eldest sister were in the background crying. All I could do was look at them and wish that I could wipe away their tears. I regretted every moment of this. I had put them through so much already and now my mother was about to lose her son to the System. I couldn't believe the verdict of the jurors.

Years later I would learn through the effort of State and Federal Appeals that the context of my guilty verdict had more to do with the prosecutor's legal scheme of overcharging the jurors with a stack of different charges than it did with my actual culpability. Yes I was responsible for pulling the trigger of a gun and causing the death of Germaine, but my actions were clearly self-defense or manslaughter, not murder. But New York State prosecutors and Courts had discovered long before my trial that by stacking several charges, by "throwing the book" at me, they gave jurors a larger palette of charges to choose from and a higher chance of some conviction. It was no longer a case of did I intend to murder Germaine or not. It was now a case of no matter what I did, do not allow me to walk off scot-free.

The Court officer walked over to me, put his hand on my shoulder and said softly, "Son, I'm sorry. We have to leave now!"

CHAPTER 38

REINVENTING MYSELF

THERE IS something stoic and impregnable about the mixture of concrete and steel when it becomes your only home for a long time. That kind of inflexibility, that unmoving, unbendable structure. I think it acts like a cocoon that holds the caterpillar in its inescapable shell. Concrete and steel all around me became my prison. But despite these walls and fences limiting my movement, I could still think and dream and imagine myself beyond the mundane existence of a concrete cell. My mind was still free, or at least I thought so. At night when the cell door closes and the inmate chatter ceases, you find yourself trapped in silence and within the confines of a less than an 8' x 8' space with nowhere to go. Fantasizing about where you could be or what you could be doing, what car you could be driving, or what you could be eating, gets tiring after a while. The fantasies become less real, less believable. Then all of a sudden I understand that prison is a metaphor. It is a metaphor about my place in the world. My thinking and behavior have hardened my mobility. I have become the concrete and steel. I am my own prison, my own cocoon, and I must either learn a way to outgrow the old me, or remain mentally and emotionally incarcerated indefinitely.

In prison you see all the time men who find it impossible to keep their desire for freedom alive. I have known men who have spent the last 20 and 30 years behind bars. Prison time had almost withered them away. They no longer had any sense or desire for freedom. They were dead men walking, accustomed to a rote pattern of prison life. There were also men, usually the younger guys, who would return a short time after being released from prison. I recall officers making bets or joking that some inmates would be back soon after their release. It was always disheartening to see freed inmates return. They would return and get right back into the program of living a prison life. For whatever reason they found it difficult to maintain their freedom on the outside. I was baffled by their recidivism. At the same time I clearly understood that freedom was not for everyone. Freedom is a responsibility that is too heavy a burden for many. That and many other factors, such as lack of family and community support, no skills and no job opportunities also played a major role in inmates returning to prison.

This became a life lesson for me. I could not stand to be humiliated all over again by going through the conveyor belt of the court and prison machine. If prison was my cocoon then I was a caterpillar destined for growth that would burst through this concrete and steel that trapped my body. Unlike some of the prisoners around me, I was determined to know the naked me, the me without the transient world of urban streets, shabby and underdeveloped ghettos, the many dark and crime ridden alleys where dealers and prostitutes make their daily living and validate their existence. I wanted to know the real me, to embrace a full human life, a humanity that had been historically denied to me and later distorted by politics, religion, pseudo-science, and media. The real me I believed was bigger than the drugs and the gangsters of my home ghetto; I was a better man than what I had become. I was determined to grow out of this environment.

A man's inner self, his true identity outside of his race and all other physical factors that give him identity in society, eventually has to become an object of study just like the material world around him.

Under the microscope of self-reflection everything begins to take shape and have meaning. Every word, every sound, every person, every experience, has value to us. In the present I could see hope for the future. A great awakening happened to me while in prison. I can't tell you when it happened. I would like to think that it happened soon after my arrival in prison. What I do know is that we are responsible for who we are today. There is no turning back to yesterday. The past is stone. And it is my past that brought me to where I found myself in prison at 16.

I remember in the beginning of my troubles, after my arrest and during my trial, I wanted so badly to undo my past to save myself from the consequences of my actions. But there was no going back. I could only move forward no matter how painful moving forward would be. The institution of prison calls this rehabilitation but rehabilitation must be self-initiated. The System by itself offers no clear direction to prisoners working toward a brighter future for their own development. Prison doesn't offer spaces for healing. There is no therapy. Change has to happen from within the prisoner, who has to be willing to wrestle with every word and sound and person and experience of his former and present lives. Change was like a speeding bullet propelled from a hidden crevasse of my mind. It raced toward the back of my eyes eventually crashing. I smelled the fresh blood, the burnt flesh, the fire and gun smoke. The aftermath left my physical sight blinded. For an unknown amount of time, all I could hear was the screeching and screaming of my past. The night sweat comes and goes, leaving me cold then hot, and then cold again until a fire comes to boil my flesh. I cringe and scream and writhe and squirm but no one hears me.

Change is silent. Change is personal. Change is painful. When the pain feels as if it can get no worse, in a dream I see myself in the place where I last left Germaine. I am covered in blood from both of us. His wounds become my own wounds and instead of inverting, the wounds protrude and I can do nothing about my life slipping away. I cannot save myself after I robbed a man of his breath and his ability to save himself. As I thought about the magnitude of what I did, of the impact I had caused, layers of my cocoon began to fall away. Prison became less a place that could contain me. Although this fatal experience would forever be part of my story, a new me was ready to look forward, leaving my past far behind.

I was only 16. I had time to work on the new me, to do my own therapy, my own reading and thinking, to grow into my mature self. I had plenty of time. I had been sentenced to prison for nine years to life, so possible parole was a long time in the future.

CHAPTER 39

WRONGLY CONVICTED

I BELIEVE that it is imperative to address the nature of my legal situation again, for it will continue to have an impact on my life. The reality of my legal situation was simple. I was not born a white American and the use of the self-defense legal justification of the popular Stand Your Ground law would never be applied to a Black teen. I was a minor in possession of an illegal loaded firearm simply because I lived in one of the most violent cities in America, and I refused to have my life snuffed out by another Black teen desperate for the satisfaction of killing one of his own kind. I hate to describe my neighborhood in such terms but it honestly was like living in a dangerous jungle. I was surrounded daily by primal rage and frustration, a raw sense of disconnect that the Black ghetto had with normal mainstream society. That disconnect stemmed from the oppression of the ghetto that the ghetto itself could never characterize or self-diagnose. It resulted in a sweeping depression across my neighborhood that was internalized by Black teens and adults and gave rise to self-medicating remedies such as drug abuse and violence throughout the city. Newburgh was a jungle and I had made a decision not to be killed as death was devouring the lives of many Black teens I knew.

What I had not known until a decade later was that the U.S. government had responded to this increasing level of Black madness by passing legislation known as the 1994 Violent Crime Control and Law Enforcement Act. This piece of legislation resulted in urban communities of color being decimated and the prison industrial complex being fueled by Black bodies, as police, prosecutors and the courts were pushed to increase Black incarceration. I would subsequently get trapped in the web of this legislative mandate despite the facts of my legal case that would have proved self-defense if I had been a white American.

Whether it was white racism exercised by the all-white district attorney, jury and judge in my case, or pressure from the legislature upon the judge to control the court, convict, and harshly sentence Black defendants, my conviction was a denial of my human right to defend my own life and the life of another person. The court had no compassion or depth of reasoning to comprehend a Black teen responding to the threat of death for his pregnant girlfriend and unborn child. The court completely ignored the unwarranted death of my unborn child. Its well-being and safety were of no relevance to the court. In a calculated way the court deducted every fact that could humanize me and normalize my response to protecting my girlfriend and child. Instead of a hero, I was a villain engaged in a gang dispute with another gang member who was deemed just as potentially violent. There was no other explanation accepted by the judge and jury.

Another interesting fact about my case was that the court, in line with the entire New York State judicial system, illegally practiced a form of prosecutorial misconduct that aimed to guarantee criminal convictions. In brief, the court was stacking the deck literally by overcharging juries with a laundry list of statutory crimes to choose from to guarantee a conviction. The prosecutor overcharged jurors to exhaust them and trick them into reaching a verdict that was favorable to the court and not fair to defendants. So in my case when I and my pregnant girlfriend were attacked by a lunatic gang member and drug dealer who had threatened to kill me for no reason, I responded to his threat by firing a handgun. The court even established that my shot had ricocheted off the pavement before striking the attacker in his carotid artery. But my case was not allowed to be a black and white clear case of self-defense. I became just another Black defendant sentenced on the sacrificial altar of the Prison Industrial Complex.

It was not until 2003 that my case reached the United States Federal Southern District Court in New York City. Justice Charles O'Brien ruled that my trial was a miscarriage of justice and an example of prosecutorial misconduct and that the trial court had conflated multiple statutory crimes together to encourage the jurors to come back with any conviction other than an acquittal. The Federal District Court ruled that the trial court had abused the law in obtaining an illegal conviction and that my conviction should be overturned. Of course the trial court would appeal the decision of the Federal District Court, and although the trial court agreed with the Federal District Court regarding the conflation of statutory crimes, the trial court argued that my defense attorney Paul Trachte, had failed to preserve these issues in the trial record. My conviction remained in effect even though the Federal Court ruled that I was a wrongly convicted man.

CHAPTER 40

A PRAYER FOR NEWBURGH

A DECADE now separates me from my city and my unfair conviction. I am still in prison and I still find myself thinking deeply and fondly of my community. Now there is some beauty within that struggle. I found myself through all of my hardship and that is a beautiful thing in itself. I am forever part of Newburgh. My story is a Newburgh story. And just as Margaret and many other friends had hope in me, had hope in my ability to change, I too have hope for the changing of a place like Newburgh. I believe that my city can change for the better when and only when we gain a sense of community and start offering love to others in everything that we do as a community. Newburgh is and has been impoverished by its lack of love. As simple and unpretentious as that may sound, it is the truth. People have lost love for one another and have lost love and trust for the institutions of that city.

Newburgh needs new inspiration from creative and forward-thinking minds that are not afraid to challenge the existing culture. The whole community needs to invest in a new mindset where people are more valuable than the infrastructure. Effective city politics cannot happen without the input of the whole community. The elders, both Black and white, must subdue their own fear of their youth and be willing to embrace young people with love and strength. They must be determined to prevent another child from succumbing to senseless street violence even if that means going out into the streets and establishing peace pacts with young people and gangs in the streets. There has to be negotiation and bargaining and a conversation between the elders and the young people. We have to offer young people opportunities to earn a living and to develop individual skills to create a more healthy city economy. We have to change the culture and make inner city life just as valuable as any other life outside the city. Most importantly, Black lives have to matter to Black people before we can even begin to have a sense of community and put an end to the fractured neighborhoods that currently exist.

Like the African proverb, "It takes a village to raise a child," it also requires hard work, and a new belief in the revival of our community for Newburgh to become once again a livable and attractive city, like Beacon just across the Hudson River revitalized by young people moving out of New York City. People must relearn what it means to be a community leader and what it means to be a responsible and accountable citizen. We must guarantee through active youth programs and available safe havens that none of our sons and daughters die an early death. We must guarantee that our children never have their minds and bodies consumed with drug use or destroy their futures by spending more wasted hours on a street corner than in a library or in school. We must stop easy access to illegal firearms and prevent some of our young people from throwing their lives away to the prison system or an early grave.

We must ensure that our streets are safe, and that no child feels their life is in so much danger that they must protect themselves by carrying a weapon, even if that requires responsible adults and the police to patrol the streets daily and build healthy relationships with every child in the neighborhood. We must see to it that our children do not become hoodlums, drug dealers, gangsters, menaces to society, and destroyers of their own community. We must see to it that creativity, a sense of achievement, and a passion for life, instead of fear and rage, hatred, and the danger of an early death, drive our children's lives. We must make sure that with all of our resources Newburgh is no longer one of the poorest and most dangerous cities in America.

CHAPTER 41

URBAN RENEWAL TRAGEDY

IF YOU want to change the world, you must first change yourself. I reminded myself of this fact everyday while I was in prison. As I was setting goals for myself, I kept the thought of being free one day fresh in my mind. It was my motivation. The thought of freedom and how I would live my new life, and all the things that I wanted to do, became a daily mantra in my life. I believed in freedom although I was still very much locked up. I was still learning about life, still very naïve about many things since I came into the System as a child of 16. If I were ever to be freed from this place, I would then be an adult with no experience at all, not even the experience of making the kind of mistakes that teenagers or young adults usually make. But life was going to come back to me full circle. I knew it. I felt it in my gut. My dreams about freedom were too vivid and too beautiful for them not to be real one day.

Time was flying by. A decade had passed since the shooting. Every day was a mental struggle to right the wrongs and to put the broken pieces of my life back together. Ten years ago at 15, the world that I was living in was extremely threatening. It was a frightening place that taught young people to survive at any cost. Kill if you have to. Rob and hustle and get over on people if you want to eat, if you want to see tomorrow. After trying to survive my ghetto jungle, I now had to live with many regrets. I wished that life came with a manual, giving instructions on how to live successfully. But it doesn't. So you live and you learn. It's all trial and error. Some survive; others don't. I thought that there is a story to be told about my survival after I have fallen. Troubled youth are going to identify with my early life and might be inspired by how I survived to make changes in their lives. Inner city teens will know all too well about a world that is spinning out of control, spinning too fast for them to hold on. They will tell us their own stories about a world that is cold and dark and deadly. They will tell us about their ghetto spaces where no child should ever have to grow up. They will use my story as a testament and validation of their own stories. We all know it is the streets that teach us violence. It is my hope that in the end young urban kids can unlearn that violence by learning to love their neighbors, by learning that violence does not have to be our weapon of protest.

I did a lot of thinking in prison. I would think about how and why a place like Newburgh could become so bleak, despondent, and disconnected. I thought about how the level of apathy was so thick, how people lived as if they were concerned only about their own survival. I wondered how people turned a blind eye to crime and violence and forced themselves to live through it. I wondered how the condition of poverty made people feel powerless and eventually desensitized to the breaking down of the community around them.

Understanding the past of Newburgh was critical to understanding my own past if I wanted to put things into perspective to affect change. What I did know was that at least two decades before I was born on June 20, 1980, Newburgh already had a slum and its Black residents, many of them from the South, were already a marginalized group bringing many social problems to the city. Welfare was allegedly attracting Southern Blacks to Newburgh. Many of these Black migrants were already poor and jobless and moving into already dilapidated sections of the city. That exacerbated the poor housing and unemployment conditions of the city, causing politicians to initiate a federal urban renewal program that demolished the modest but livable spaces of Blacks and forced them to relocate to older housing in the inner city of Newburgh.

In one striking blow of a policy to renew some areas of Newburgh, historic Black sections were demolished during the 1960s. What remained was blocks of rubble and explosive tension between the Black community and white politicians over broken promises. Displaced families waited for the promises of city government to be fulfilled. The promise was a federal redevelopment of what the city had destroyed, but no rebuilding ever happened and the promises were never kept by the city.

Large sections of the Black community developed an apathy and a distrust of city officials that exists to this day. Black ghetto anger easily translated into a mimicking of the level of destruction that whites had already executed in older Black neighborhoods. Black people felt robbed and in return started to put the community's interest last. Black housing and streets began to reflect the disconnect between the Black community and the dominant white culture and between Black people themselves. Neighborhood neglect, apolitical attitudes and irresponsibility were now common in the Black community, which would fester and eventually create a culture where Blacks were unlikely to participate in public affairs, even those concerning their own destiny.

In the following three decades, from the 1970s to 1990s, the condition of Newburgh's Black ghetto did not improve. Money and job opportunities were scarce. This opened up the opportunity for the drug market and low level crime to take root within the Black community and to become the means by which a lot of Black people survived. The ghetto became synonymous with widespread unemployment, academic dropout and low life expectations, drug culture and rising crime. By the 1990s the Latino community began to make a presence in the city and due to language and culture barriers, strife resulted between the new Latin population and the already existing Black community. It seemed that after the urban renewal disaster of the 1960s, Newburgh was destined to become another "urban renewal" slum within the American landscape. What future Black generations like my own would inherit was a ruthless attitude, an aptitude for self-destructive behavior, and low expectations for life achievements.

My generation was the generation of Niggas With Attitude, a West Coast rapper group, and Tupac, and Gangster Rap. The culture taught us that it was all about sagging jeans, gangs, guns, and taking from others without asking. We simply felt abandoned and as if the larger society didn't care about us, so we stopped caring about ourselves. Most of the Black people we could look at every day, if they weren't in jail or deceased, were clear casualties of drug wars and neutralizing efforts by the government to destabilize the Black community. We didn't see anything meaningful or prideful in the lives of those who came before us. When we found ourselves able to sell crack to our elders and witnessed how adults failed to keep clean their own front stoop and blocks, all respect for our elders was long gone. I found myself surrounded by years of pent-up rage and frustration that had no outlet to express itself. Newburgh had already lost its sense of community. Prominent Black businesses were replaced by outsiders. The Black dollar had no way of remaining in the Black community because Blacks had nothing to offer in terms of service or merchandise. The more lack of opportunity grew, the greater the rise of poverty and disconnect from the neighborhood. Dilapidation or property damage increased the presence of police and police always made us feel like we were second and third class citizens in our own neighborhoods. I was trapped just like every other young Black male, with very little hope of ever escaping this grim city alive. And the tragedy of it all, I now understand, was that many of us would rather succumb to death at an early age than to live through the ugly poverty that was Newburgh.

CHAPTER 42

BECOMING A CHANGED MAN

IT HAS been two years since my last parole hearing in 2005. It felt like this moment was never going to come back around. Over a decade in the System and no longer a troubled teenager, I was about to meet the Parole Commissioners for a second time. The residue of former Governor Pataki's hard on crime politics was still lingering up in Albany the first time I saw the parole board. So I was denied my freedom based on the nature of my crime— the victim had died, regardless of the mitigating circumstances of the crime. Two years ago the parole commissioners were honest enough to acknowledge that I had made many strides toward personal change during my incarceration, but that because the victim had lost his life my freedom was not yet possible. I understood that. I understood that Germaine had lost his life on that terrible night in June some ten years ago because of a confrontation where I ended up firing a handgun. No matter how badly I wished that night had never happened, I could not change it. I could never bring Germaine back to life. He didn't deserve to die. My unborn child still in the womb of my girlfriend Mecca didn't deserve to die. Germaine and I didn't deserve to be in a confrontation on that rainy night where one of us would die and the other would spend years of his life behind bars. We were both young teenagers and in the same circumstances of living in the ghetto and learning all the wrong ways to live and to handle problems. We thought of violent solutions first before anything else and lived out that violence, even at the expense of losing our own lives.

But the ghetto wasn't at this 2007 parole hearing, neither was Newburgh. It was I who had to change and had to demonstrate first to myself that I was a changed person. What Newburgh had made of me some ten years ago, a reactionary and impulsive killer, did no longer exist within me. That person, child or not, was unfit to be free in a society where all people had a right not to live in fear of losing their lives. I knew that I was no longer that person. In fact, that was not who I wanted to be in the first place. I was only responding to an environment that taught me to either kill or be killed. That thinking and my response were all wrong. I was above and beyond that now. I had found my humanity and discovered self-love. It was now my responsibility to show not just the parole board my new character but also the city which had made me hate myself and other Blacks.

I am a different person now. I have transcended and matured. I am now a teacher of my own experience and know the value of sharing my experience because there are Black youth out there who are feeling exactly how I once felt. Even deeper, there are Black people who suffer from self-hate, Blacks who find themselves victims of negative attitudes and values directed toward all people of color. They have no filters in place against these negative attitudes and end up inflicting these attitudes and values on their own kind. Black violence is spawned by a lack of Black love. This is what I believe. This is what I know. Black people live within a system of white cultural supremacy and political hegemony. That is the reality that shapes and fuels Black existence in our society. But a lack of education and Black ignorance facilitate our own destruction. Only Black love, respect and concern for other Blacks can counter these negative forces.

In a few hours I will meet the Parole Commissioners once again. Although I probably should be nervous, I am free from fear and anxiety. There is nothing that the Parole Board can do to me that will damage the person that I have become. Granting me freedom is in their power but I already experience freedom because I am no longer the person who lived and thought the way I did as a teenager. I am free of the old me, no longer incarcerated within that mental prison of hate and self-doubt. Violence is no longer a weapon of my choice. If I earn my freedom it is because I have changed so much that this cage can no longer hold me captive. I believe I am beyond what the System could offer me at this moment. Yes, I was once that 15-year-old teenager who was so hopeless about my situation that I responded with violence and took someone's life. I had defended myself with an illegal gun and Germaine was dead as a result. I own that decision and have taken responsibility for it and always will. I cannot change my past but I can continue working to change my future.

I cannot convince the Parole Board about anything they cannot see radiating from my being. All of my accomplishments in prison are written down for the commissioners to read. That, however, is not what my or anyone's freedom should be based upon. Instead I want them to understand my compassion and remorse for what I did and to understand the reasons for my thinking at that time. I want them to see that I understand the dynamic of my reckless thinking when I was continually attacked by another human being. I want them to hear my hope, to believe my hope that I can make a positive difference back home. That I can go back home to my old neighborhood that I once considered a war zone and tell my story to other young Blacks. My story can possibly prevent them from ending up dead or trapped in the system. I am hopeful because my life now has a purpose that I believe in.

In the end, I do not want to be remembered as the Black kid from the ghetto who shot and killed another Black youth and threw his own life away. I do not want to be remembered as another Black man who was once in prison. I want to be remembered for overcoming and enduring and struggling through years of facing the demons within myself and eventually freeing myself from my own cocoon. I want to be remembered for surviving Newburgh. I used my tragic experience as a catalyst to change my philosophy, thinking, and attitude. In the beginning I was no better than the city that made me. I lived by certain bad rules for surviving the city and they had cost me my freedom and another person his life. Today I am a man. I am a Black man. I am a new man.

CHAPTER 43

NEW BEGINNINGS

THE MOMENT arrived when I was to appear before the Parole Board for the second time. I spent the whole night rehearsing key points of my development that I needed the Parole Board to hear. I thought about what questions the Commissioners would have for me and how I would respond convincingly. Much of what was said that morning has slipped my memory. The only thing I remember is that I was going to be released from prison this time. I was certain of this. It was a feeling of conviction. I had spent ten long years dissecting and developing my life. I found ways to rip my young life apart and to be brutally honest with myself and about the society that I was raised in. I knew that my change was sincere because I was totally uncomfortable with the older version of myself. The man that I am today is against the cultural attitudes and beliefs once held by the old me. They weren't going to deny me freedom. I was already a free man. I was no longer a prisoner in my own mind, imprisoned by the faulty thinking and reasoning of the streets. The confines of these four walls around me were no longer enough to hold me down. Freedom was just a moment away. It wasn't a reward for my good behavior in prison. It was the result of me freeing myself from those thoughts and urban ideologies that were detrimental to a free society and existence.

Unlike the first time I went before the Parole Board where there were a handful of us, I was the only prisoner to be seen by the Parole Commissioners that day. It was strange and very uncommon but I didn't think much about it. An officer came to escort me from the Annex where I was housed at the Green Haven Maximum Facility where the Parole Board was meeting. The whole vibe was totally different from the last time. I was told to sit outside on a wooden bench and wait to be called in. I was calm and at peace. Those butterflies in my stomach that existed two years before at my first parole hearing where not there this time around. I knew that everything was going to be all right. I had worked diligently for the past ten years for this moment and believed that the universe and fate would not conspire against me. This would be my last time ever seeing a parole board.

"Nasihah Jones, are you ready to be seen by the Parole Commission?" It felt like I had waited an eternity for this moment. Of course, I'm ready, I thought to myself. "Yes sir!" I replied to the same guard who had escorted me here. "I am ready for freedom!"

I stood up from the hard wooden bench, gave myself a good stretch, looked back once or twice at everything that was my world for the past ten years, and began to stride into the room where the parole hearing was being held, all the way to my freedom. Freedom was finally right here before me. It was now a tangible reality that I would be able to touch and taste and know again. I am an adult now so freedom will look very different to me. And even if I do decide to go back to my old city of Newburgh, I will return as a new man with a story to tell. The past I will never be able to change. I am content with that fact. Soon I will have so much to look forward to that the past will be visited only as a reminder of what I survived. I am sure that my future will have new obstacles and challenges that I will have to deal with but now I will be prepared for whatever comes my way. I just want to hug my mother and smell the fresh air far from any prison. Maybe I'll go visit a park or two and eat something that I haven't had in over ten years.

I will definitely visit the museums Margaret took me to as a child and remember her intentional humanity towards me. Sadly Margaret died four years before my release from prison. Her untimely death in 2003 was devastating. I had lost my second mother and mentor. I lost my life coach and the very first person to ever believe in me when I didn't believe in myself. Margaret was not able to see me walk out of prison a free man but I am sure that she already knew that this day would eventually arrive.

After 11 long years, from a teen to a young man, my incarceration came to an end. The Parole Commissioners were unanimously satisfied with my transformation and they believed in my vision of how I would lead a positive life on the outside. This nightmare was finally over. I was free from the prison that cut short a man's pathway to the future. I was free from the self-doubt and fear that once confined me as a teen and that paralyzed my ability to be courageous in my neighborhood.

CHAPTER 44

FIRST FRESH AIR

STEPPING OUTSIDE of prison on May 15, 2007 for the first time after 11 years, I just stood at the entrance of the Green Haven Correctional Facility and reflected deeply about my new relationship with fresh air and open space and the unfettered objects around me. In that moment, in those few seconds outside the smell of brick, metal, and stale indoor prison air, I already appreciated my physical freedom. Prison can institutionalize you and rally screw up your sense of reality. It can have you forgetting all the small things that constitute the beauty of life, things that we usually take for granted. Prison can make you feel like you are undeserving of a cool breeze and natural sun light. It's all ego in that place and a struggle to preserve the ego. We easily begin to disassociate from liberty and begin to carve out this artificial existence of surviving with 24-hour surveillance in small prison cells. We make a life in a small confined space or at least we think we do. And this goes on for years and it becomes normal to us until we forget the sounds of streams and babies cooing. We romanticize liberation from prison only to think about the old versions of ourselves in old contexts. Fantasizing and rehashing our past lives. Prisoners become stuck in their pasts, even though time is still moving. I am thankful that I've always had support from the outside that helped to prevent institutionalization. I've met so many prisoners who have lost their minds and could not regain their natural sensibilities. Behind bars is a different world and to survive, I admit, I pushed a lot of feelings that applied to being free to the back of my memory. But on the outside now, I realized how much I had missed those feelings. I understood what it felt like to be human again.

I didn't concern myself with any of the social stigmas that follow the formerly incarcerated. I knew my story of how I ended up incarcerated and understood that my greatest mission was not to prove to others that I was not a threat. My mission was to continue my redemption by becoming my greatest self and being a light of inspiration to those men and women, boys and girls, who have fallen into their darkness. Had I been lucky enough I would have had a different set of parents, and I would have grown up in a different neighborhood and had greater life opportunities. But that is not how life dealt me my cards. Adversity made me strong and made me who I am. Incarceration pushed me to know myself and in doing so I overcame my fear of accepting that I am too strong to be limited. My supporters and I had fought long for this day; Margaret especially had given so much of herself to see me out of that cage. I was prepared for the world. I was walking out of prison awake with a new set of eyes and ears. I knew where I wanted to be and what I wanted to accomplish in my life.

Of course the sad part about returning home is that I was leaving behind so many people I had come to know on the inside. Some of those brothers are my comrades and the wisest teachers in my education. I knew that I was never going to see most of them ever again. That was a depressing thought, even now as I think about it. But it was another reality that I came to grips with the minute I stepped off those prison grounds. Some of my comrades were never coming home to their families and they were never going to have the luxury of recreating a life for themselves without the poverty and the trauma plagued conditions that fostered their poor decisions early in life.

CHAPTER 45

OUT ON PAROLE

PAROLE WAS something that I could not accept right after my release from prison. Parole Officers seemed driven by their authority to send a parolee back to prison at will, especially if the parolee made the slightest mistake. I had already walked on eggshells while in prison trying to avoid confrontation with the prison guards, knowing that it made their day to send a prisoner into the hole of solitary confinement and to write them an infraction slip. Any negative encounter with guards could easily damage a prisoner's chance of being granted parole, as if a prisoner's conviction wasn't bad enough already. And now Parole Officers had that same power of denying me my God-given right to freedom. I was not willing to play their game the way they wanted me to play it.

The idea of being sent back to prison made me fearful. In the first few days out of prison I literally would have nightmares about parole and police officers hovering over me with their guns drawn trying to send me back to prison. I recall thinking how parallel the prison experience was to slavery, mostly disenfranchised men and women from disenfranchised neighborhoods, condemned to prison sentences and stripped of all of their earthly possessions. I remember that awful prison bus ride when all of the prisoners were chained to one another and sent off to various facilities upstate. Each one of us came from different parts of the State of New York and although we didn't know one another, circumstances bonded us by race and the common denominator that we all were going to be away from our families for a long time. I later found out these upstate prison communities received economic benefits for housing prisoners. So, many mouths were fed from the misfortune of prisoners. Even the U.S. Constitution still supported the institution of slavery via prison. So by no means was I ever going back there, and I didn't plan on being confined by parole restrictions for long either.

My plan for success was to enroll in college since academia was where I had already found comfort. I had already amassed many college credits from professional and correspondence studies I did while still in prison. I was pretty good at writing and articulating my ideas. And despite having been confined, I still managed to build a pretty impressive academic portfolio for myself that would work in my favor when I eventually applied to colleges. I was clear in my belief that a college degree would give me leverage against "a felon" that would always be attached to my name. I had heard stories of ex-felons not getting hired because of their criminal records. And I had seen enough of those men forced back into unlawful activities that increased the high prison recidivism rate (40% in New York State).

CHAPTER 46

A NEW BLACK MODEL

MY LIFE sentence did not mean that I would spend the rest of my life in prison. After making parole and being on the outside now, my life sentence didn't mean that I would have to be on parole for the rest of my life either. The fact that I had decided to handle my freedom in a very unconventional way freed my parole officers from the burden of having to supervise me. The vast majority of former prisoners are unlikely to get out of prison, enroll in college immediately and reinvent their lives back to normalcy. My life as a teen was far from normal, but having a decade of solitude and introspection to work on becoming the man I wanted to be allowed me to plan the kind of life I would live once out of prison. My parole officers had not expected me, a parolee, to pursue the route of education.

Besides that, my life sentence as a teenager for what was clearly self-defense was as confusing to my parole officer as it had been to the many prison counselors who had to review my case as I was returning to the general population. That was the standard reaction. My parole officer thought that under the circumstances of my case I probably should not have been convicted of murder when all of the facts clearly described an act of self-defense. And if a conviction was unavoidable, then certainly I should not have been given such a lengthy prison sentence. In spite of how the parole officer and many prison counselors before him may have felt, their feelings about my case didn't get me out of prison any sooner, and their opinions were not going to get me off parole easily either.

I ended up being on parole for a little over two years—despite my life sentence. The Parole Commission just didn't see any purpose in sending parole officers to a college campus to ensure that I was doing the right thing. I was a college student and fully engaged in academic activities. My past as far as I was concerned was long behind me and buried. I was embracing my new life as a college student and living just as freely as the professors and other students around me. I refused to define myself as an ex-con and therefore didn't think and act as if I was ever in prison. All that convinced the Parole Commission to decide that further parole supervision was not necessary.

Much of my success on the outside depended upon my attitude and positive thinking. I remembered so many of my teenage peers rushing violently towards death. A decade later the survivors of the deadly 90s and this new generation of Black adolescents that I was witnessing on all the old ghetto blocks where I once hung out were still caught up in the cycle of premature violent death or prison. I thought constant funerals in the city should be a riveting lesson about what being out in the streets led to. I saw that some of my Black brothers were already victims of the mass incarceration initiatives of the 80s and 90s. Realizing that these obvious truths weren't so obvious, and that many of my brothers were akin to black flies trapped in a spider's web, forced to fashion a culture of survival around imminent death and inter-racial genocide, I knew that it was in my best interest not to let any of my new energy of freedom get wasted in a nihilistic and defeatist attitude. Keeping my positive energy level up was vital to my success.

The memory of Margaret Johns was also my daily reminder that I had come too far from my old life to give up now. She had seen something good in me a long time ago, and even during my darkest hours, she had remained loyal and committed to the goodness in my real self. One day I was going to be free, but more than that I was going to exercise all of the positive lessons I had learned along the way. I was determined to walk through new doors and create new chapters in my life. I was going to travel and make new friends, I was going to fall in and out of love, find and be found by love. One day I was going to have a decent life.

On at least two occasions I have been asked by Bobby Smith, the Director of the Goshen, NY, Secure Center, to share my story with the incarcerated youth there. I was honored because Bobby and several other employees in that facility knew me and watched me grow up during my stay there. I also believed that it was important for these youth to hear the story of someone who once wore the same juvenile detention uniform and sneakers. If I could make it out, they could too. They just needed some encouragement, some inspiration, someone to tell them that they are more than hoodlums and society's fuck ups.

Black adolescents need new Black models to define new possibilities for becoming better human beings. Current nomenclature for defining the varieties of Black adolescence experience, and Blackness itself, are dead end in nature. The word Nigga, a variation of the word Nigger, still robs Black people of their humanity. It not only demeans the very essence of what Black people have meant to this planet, but also stifles their psychological and linguistic ability to deal with their ancestors' catastrophic moment of enslavement by Europeans and white colonialists. Even now, 400 years later, Black people are still *Niggas*, not because the rapper Jay Z used that word, but because the nature of their attachment to that word has imprisoned them in a continual second-class citizenry. I remind young people who I work with that not only is America still racist, but that young Black people are still charged with the job of changing American attitudes toward Blacks. If that sounds impossible, then first change yourself. Change how you define yourself and begin to understand the relationship of

Black people to existing white institutions. Learn the history of the world and study the historical trends that brought us to where we are today. Understand the adversarial forces that want to erase and subjugate Black and brown people. Get educated and empower yourself with skills you need to survive.

I remind them that education is not a right in this society. It is a privilege and therefore it becomes a weapon. Wherever people of color find themselves, in juvenile jail facilities, on the streets, or on college campuses, they must gain as much education as they can. Our lack of knowledge about ourselves and our history has been our great loss over the past four centuries, caused by our lack of access to information, good education and good job opportunities.

I tell young people that Black races were not always slaves, and the victims of police and other forms of systemic oppression. The Black race in both ancient and pre-colonial times, maintained kingdoms and vast empires in Africa. European colonial powers increased their presence in Africa, and their colonies worked to eliminate Black wealth and stability. Blacks were defeated and enslaved. They weren't already slaves. They were forced into slavery. And then narratives were invented by Europeans to justify Black slavery and Black degradation. This degradation was used to exploit us and erase our history.

But somehow we continued to survive. I tell them a story about a young Black boy who came from nothing. His mother was poor and his dad was absent. He attended grade school as other children his age did. And under the influence of white teachers he was taught a narrative that his history began with slavery and because of the relationship that Blacks had with slavery, nothing great was expected from him. Those same teachers concluded that he and others like him would never amount to anything, that prison and death, like those preceding four centuries of slavery and oppression were the only viable options for him. Such benighted teachers wrote and reiterated a narrative that limited the imagination of that Black boy and many of his peers. No one told them anything different or challenged the narratives of those teachers, so those Black children believed their every word, crippling and stifling any possibility for them to rise above the contrived realities of their racist teachers.

I teach my Black students that historical narratives can change, that Black people have the power to be transformed and to rewrite the narratives that support the realities of their oppression. I was once that Black boy buried in lies and false myths of Blackness and Black manhood in my public school classrooms. Those lies made me paranoid as I believed the worst about myself and other Blacks. I had lived with that insanity in my ghetto—that insanity still exists--until I was consumed by it and condemned to a life sentence at 16 years of age. That was my story, but it is not my only story. It is not the conclusion of my story. In prison I discovered a way to survive the erasure of my Black being by the system. And I discovered myself. I learned how to rewrite my own narrative and to take responsibility for my own identity and my own destiny.

I know now that I am much more than an ex-convict. I am greater than the gangbangers and gangsters who damaged my youth. I am greater than any one bad personal experience that others will use to define me. I am greater than the myths and distortions of Blackness. I am a man. I am a new man. I am the black salt of this earth.

CHAPTER 47

NEWBURGH UNCHANGED

I WAS fresh back home in Newburgh. Margaret's two step daughters, Beatrice and Lisa Stern, had picked me up from Greene Haven and had decided to give me a tour of my old Newburgh neighborhood before they would introduce me to my new apartment in Cornwall, NY, a small mostly white town in the suburbs of Newburgh. I sat in the front seat of Beatrice's Subaru and stared pensively out of the window at the same Newburgh streets that I once walked up and down every day as a kid. Nothing had changed in ten years. Even the people looked the same and were surprisingly doing the exact same things they were doing before I left. I felt like I was looking out of a one-way window, hoping that nobody could see me staring at the crowds of people standing on corners and on their porches, and wondering for a quick second if this was all a dream—that I actually had not been removed for over a decade from my home streets.

Gentrification had not yet come to Newburgh so the properties and buildings were still in as bad shape as the people were. Maybe in that moment I was experiencing delusions of grandeur because I wrongly assumed that I had the streets all figured out and that I was going to come back here and change things. It appeared that people had not evolved from the insanity of the 1990s in Newburgh. I couldn't believe that some Black folk were still smoking crack and young Black men were still selling crack. Both unfortunate predicaments I understood to be an outgrowth of the systemic oppression of poverty. I really had imagined that the scene in my neighborhood would be improved. There was a younger generation out there now and they had inherited the Bloods and Crips namesake and adopted the perpetuation of violence. Most of these new bangers were the younger siblings of the older guys I grew up with. The 1990s hadn't left anything constructive for the neighborhood so gang banging was the only attractive option for these kids. From time to time I would visit Newburgh on the weekends or during my holiday breaks from college and I would attempt to talk to many of the young homies. My youngest brother and several of his friends were Bloods and they were always around my mother's house. So I would use those moments to bond with them and offer them knowledge. I understood not to tread upon their lifestyle to the degree that I came off as disrespectful. To an outsider, groups of young Black men united are a gang, but to those who know, these gangs were a family and were all they had. Their unity I thought was a beautiful accomplishment. But their level of violence and crime was getting out of hand and had the entire community enraged and frightened. Around 2012 a reporter by the name of Doyle Murphy from the Times Herald-Record began reporting the gang activity in Newburgh. Several families that had lost their children to gun violence decided to allow Doyle into their homes to get their emotional reflections on having a child murdered by way of gang violence. Week after week stories about Newburgh's gang violence were hitting the Record's front page. Doyle Murphy had figured out a way to weave random and isolated crimes together to create this web of gang violence terrorizing the streets of Newburgh. From the beginning, I disagreed with that understanding and clearly understood what Doyle was up to.

It seemed that this reporter was creating propaganda with an agenda to alert the federal government to come into Newburgh to initiate a mass incarceration of known and alleged gang members. I was against inner-city crime and against youth killing youth but I opposed the idea of sweeping indictments that would lead to the incarceration of many of the young males in my neighborhood. There had to be a different approach. Mass incarceration would only result in further disenfranchisement of my community. I would spend many weeks out in the community, beside Timothy Hayes-El and another community advocate, James Thorpe, attempting to connect with as many young people as possible to warn them of the legal dangers of organized crime. I would eventually write a Community Survival Guide aimed at gang members in the city of Newburgh that could educate them on Federal RICO charges, the consequences of gang culture, and ways that young people can shift their negative energy into positive community contributions. Unfortunately, my guide book did not reach enough hands and was not strong enough to slow down the negative momentum of gang banging and the quickly approaching federal intervention. The authorities would eventually arrive and fulfill everything that my guide book had predicted. A total of three federal raids were enough to eliminate a large portion of Newburgh's Black males between the ages of 18 and 35. That whole experience had taught me that my approach to saving youth although genuine, was ineffective and too philosophic.

I did not have a lot of money or resources to bring large changes to my neighborhood. But I had a wealth of knowledge that I believed could inspire the whole community. But I was being too idealistic. I had just returned home from my own incarceration. I had much to learn. Before I could do anything to help others, I had to first help myself and figure out what I was going to do with my sudden freedom, and how I was going to find a job.

CHAPTER 48

NETWORK OF FRIENDS

MY TRANSITION from prison to freedom was relatively easy because I had established a network of friends on the outside who were willing to support me in my return to a world I had been exiled from. These friends believed in my good nature. Margaret Stern had convinced them of that in her many campaigns to rally support for me. They were also people concerned with criminal justice issues and prison reform, and I was a young man who had obviously been railroaded by the judicial system, and who had educated himself during his prison sentence to become an asset to others once out. I was preparing myself for life outside and trying to do the necessary character building work to prevent recidivism.

My self-development work to prevent the paralyzing victim mentality that seizes so many prisoners prepared me to accept and make good use of help from my supporters. Friends such as Richard "RJ" Smith, the leading real estate broker in Orange County, NY, and Beatrice and Lisa Stern, step-daughters of Margaret, believed in me enough to open doors of opportunity for me and help me come back to normal life. It was RJ who helped me get into my first college after prison, Orange County Community College, where I would make such an academic impression on the Sciences Department that they would send me to a Summer Research Program at the four-year

SUNY campus in Purchase, NY, where I would eventually receive my Bachelors Degree. Without the support of RJ who understood my needs and talents and knew exactly who to reach out to, I would have had a much more difficult time navigating toward a successful freedom.

One professor at Orange County Community College (OCCC) who took a paternal liking to me was Jim Givant, professor of English and Philosophy. While I was still in prison, RJ Smith arranged a pilot program for Professor Givant to teach me college English and Philosophy credit courses by reading great literature and writing essays about it. After my release from prison, I continued studying with Professor Givant as a regular student at OCCC, and he generously offered me a place to stay at his home. He also edited early drafts of this memoir which I had begun while still in prison in 2005.

In fact, I can candidly say that had it not been for the inspiration that RJ and Bea and her sister, Lisa Stern, and many others gave me, I would not have had the personal courage to want a new life that was so diametrically different from the earlier ghetto life that I suffered. My new friends were more than just advisors to me. They were good models and instructors, hardworking people who believed in social causes and community outreach and raising children in healthy environments. They were teaching me how to live with a sense of selfless humanity that had been absent from both prison and the ghetto of Newburgh. In my new found freedom, with my new vision of what was possible for myself, I was able for the first time to live without fear of being shot dead or robbed and had a consortium of good people around me giving me positive direction.

Bea and Lisa Stern introduced me to an organic farmer by the name of Guy Jones who gave me my first job as a farmer in the Black Dirt onion growing area of Orange County, NY. Farming had not been my ideal job but it was my first assurance that I would be just fine as long as I came to work and did my job, whatever it was. Farming in rich black soil was a job that I would not want to do again in my life. For starters, I had no idea how extremely dirty farming could be. Every day after work I would arrive home covered in an extra layer of black and washing the dirt away created mud in my tub. Secondly, I was the only Black farmer working alongside Mexicans who didn't speak English at all, or I should say that I didn't speak Spanish at all since I was clearly the minority person in that situation. Working with these Mexican laborers was enlightening because of their work ethic, integrity, and their oneness with the soil and vegetation. I had never seen anything like that. They were hard laborers but elegantly moved about the earth with no superficial pride. They genuinely respected their work and took pride in completing an honest day's work. I didn't stay at this job very long but I did walk away from that black soil with an appreciation for hard work and an understanding that farming was an introductory job that I needed to do before I could graduate to more complex academic and work demands.

About that time I met Jim Ottaway, a good friend of Margaret and her husband, Peter Stern, chairman of the Storm King Art Center.

I could never fully describe how much support Jim Ottaway has been for my life over the past decade or so. He joined the circle of supporters Margaret petitioned to help get justice for my case, or to get the court or the Parole Board to release me. These supporters understood that my murder charge was unjustified and was prosecuted unfairly, that it was a clear case of self-defense, and that there was an obvious miscarriage of justice, from the prosecution's misrepresentation of my witnesses' testimony to my conviction and long sentence.

My circle of supporters all happened to be white. They unanimously agreed that had I been born white and in similar circumstances, a totally different legal outcome would have been the result. They did not just have pity for a young Black boy from the ghetto, nor did they decide to help my fight for freedom in a random act of white goodness. The truth of the matter was that most of my defenders had known me or about me since I was eight years old, and they saw me as a bright-minded artistic young child who had the potential to become anything that he wanted to be if he could survive the overwhelming challenges that would come from growing up in a neighborhood plagued with systemic poverty and crime.

I met Jim Ottaway after Margaret's death in October, 2003, right after I got out of prison in July, 2007. He wanted me to know that he fully supported me and would pick up where Margaret had left off. At the time I had imagined Margaret's shoes being too big to be filled by anyone. Margaret was more than just my friend. She was a mother to me and had showered me with a kind of love that was dramatically different from the love I had received from my parents or grandparents or my juvenile relations with girls before my arrest. But Jim kept his word as a good man. Not only did he try to convince the Parole Board to grant my release, writing that my further incarceration would be unjust and a contradiction of New York State penal policy of rehabilitation of its legally condemned, he also continued to work with me throughout the years after prison to ensure that my transition and navigation to a new life would be successful. It was this kind of support from Jim Ottaway that pushed me later to move to the nation's capital.

CHAPTER 49

IMAGINATION

COLLEGE WAS something that most formerly incarcerated people never think about. The majority of prisoners assume that college is not an option or that their lives are usually so broken after prison that they just think about trying to get a job and place to live to satisfy the conditions of their parole. But for me, I used to romanticize about attending college. I would visualize the whole college experience quite often while in prison – fantasizing my room in juvenile detention and later my prison cell being replaced by an actual classroom where I was learning and articulating grand ideas rather than wrestling to communicate with fellow prisoners who still used street jargon to define their current experience, if they thought about that at all. I had no template for going to college or even where to begin but I knew that is where I was going to go after my incarceration. I would be the first of my mother's children to go to college. When I was growing up, any conversation about going to college was unheard of. My parents didn't conceive of college as a viable option to make it out of the ghetto. None of my friend's parents were having that conversation with them either. I never once heard the word "college" mentioned by my high school teachers. So the neighborhood became a dead end in my imagination and I assumed it was the same for most men and women who were incarcerated in their teens. But reading books and feeling creative enough to imagine newer spaces for myself, and believing in personal change, I just knew that I would find a way to attend and graduate from college. College was going to be my way of rewriting the assumption that after incarceration a prisoner has only one option and that option is to return to prison.

I understood early in my prison time that I did not want to be back in the streets without a plan. I was too young before prison to have developed a hustle to earn a dollar, and I knew that I was now too educated to get released and become a drug dealer or any other type of criminal. I did not want to have to adopt that street "hustling mentality" to survive my new chance at freedom. I had been a witness to that mentality and witnessed more failure than success. Everyone in the streets had a hustle. Those who did not, were searching for one. That is how you eat and how your kids eat. The hustle is always about turning nothing into something. We all dream about escaping the ghetto and we believe that our hustles will be our way out. In reality, so few people are ever thinking outside of their box and even fewer are thinking about long-term investments like a college education. They just don't have that language in their vocabulary. I was in the same predicament before my incarceration. I was confined to a limited world that was structured out of Ebonics (a Black dialect) and the imagination of what white folks thought about people of color. There was no freedom around us. Poverty was a prison and so was the ghetto. How we spoke lacked self-determination. Our own tongues prevented us from imaging better lives for ourselves and for our children. Had I known better, I would probably have chosen to do better. We were epistemologically non-emancipated.

Many of us perceived the world only as it was handed to us. We were not inventors of a new language and new experiences. We did not see the world as a thing to change and to fit who and what we represented. The world was antithetical to us and we somehow found ourselves in it and made the best of it. We thought that the world did not love us, but we expected others to love us when we failed to love ourselves.

My incarceration at 15 became an opportunity for me to open my eyes and to peel back the veil of self-doubt and miseducation that placed me in that crisis of my life. I was using my own legal situation in prison as a philosophical exercise in search of truth. I would question my life purpose after having shot another young Black teen. And because I did think of myself as a victim of circumstance, it increased by thirst and hunger to find meaning in my life. And that was my whole plan during my incarceration – to think and to question and to think some more until things became clear. I realized that on the outside in my community we were told not to question our existence. Just deal with life as it crushes you. The men around me in the various prisons I spent time in, many of them were being crushed by that same force and they were losing their vitality as time went on. I wasn't going to become one of them and be crushed by time and prison. So I did my sentence as a college student and didn't allow prison guards or other prisoners to define my prison experience for me. If I was able to astro project myself out of prison as a matriculated student in college, then it was possible for me to be an educated man in the real world, free at least from my ghetto neighborhood.

CHAPTER 50

AFTER SUNY PURCHASE

MY FINAL year as a student at the State University of New York at Purchase, NY, was coming to an end. Come May, 2009, I would be walking across that stage with a Bachelors Degree in my hand. Not one of my professors nor the many friends I made at Purchase could imagine that just two years earlier I was walking out of a very different institution, still young enough to attend college and readjust my life quite swiftly. Not knowing how people would judge me, it was important to keep my past incarceration a secret. I did not want to walk around the campus with the social stigma that came with having been convicted and incarcerated. As far as I was concerned that was all very much behind me and I wanted my existence not to be defined by my murder conviction.

At the same time I knew that I was committed to issues of prison reform and the enormous community and personal dysfunction that happened way before my incarceration. That connection allowed me to pursue college internships with organizations such as NYPIRG and Community Voices Heard where I would lead campaigns to fight against hunger and homelessness in New York City, and I would work to empower an immigrant community in Yonkers to know their rights against slum landlords. One year as co-president of the Black Student Union, my friend Josh and I had the organization compose letters to be mailed off to incarcerated political prisoners in the United States, pledging our support as college students. So I was very much still interested in prison issues and had not run away from my own experience. I just believed that my past was better off in the past, until the time was right to disclose my story.

After I graduated from SUNY Purchase I decided to leave my apartment in the Bronx, NY, and move back upstate to Newburgh to work alongside Community Activist Timothy Hayes-El. I became interested in Hayes-El's work in my home community after reading several articles about him in the local newspaper. He had become an articulate spokesperson about the plight of his city and an advocate for Newburgh's youth. I had known Hayes-El from my youth and remembered him as one of the older guys in the neighborhood who was a force to reckon with. Hayes-El was a reformed criminal turned activist who truly cared about the community. People either loved him or they hated him. But he remained solid and authentic when it came to turning young people's lives around. The El affixed to his last name came from his affiliation with the Moorish Science Temple and the assertion that American Blacks were actually descendants of 15th Century African Moors and indigenous tribes that were present in the Americas before the arrival of Columbus and other European colonialists, and not all descendants of enslaved Africans brought to America via the Trans-Atlantic Slave Trade.

Hayes-El and I worked together on several projects in the city. He had a burning commitment to the City of Newburgh that I was never quite able to adopt. I was the more pessimistic one when it came to change in my city. But despite my justified pessimism, I had real skill sets and experience in community organizing. I also owned a few digital cameras and thought of my cameras as weapons of radical change. I would spend the next seven years of my friendship with Hayes-El documenting his life on camera. He was a living testament to personal transformation in my opinion, leaving behind his gangster ways and adopting peaceful methods of community change and advocacy for people with no voice to speak for themselves. If he was not at City Council meetings fighting for decent wage employment and more employment opportunities, he would write Marcus Mosiah Garveyesque poems lamenting the suffering of his community and the need for self-love and self-knowledge. I was able to capture his journey as an activist in a documentary I produced right before he died in 2014. The documentary, "The 9th Terror: A Love/Hate Relationship With Newburgh," was a project that I worked on in the fall of 2014. It aimed to capture the raw voice of a silent community, and it articulated community tragedy through an artistic expose`. Hayes-El was my best friend and a comrade. He made my time spent in Newburgh after prison and college feel meaningful. It felt like we were making changes in that city and getting Black people to take on local politics and politicians. His death came unexpectedly during his campaign for a seat on the City Council. A few years after his passing, the City of Newburgh would rename Lander Street "Hayes-El Way" in his memory.

CHAPTER 51

REVISITING MY CITY

OVER THE years since I got out of prison I have often revisited my old hometown of Newburgh to meet old friends and family. Not much has changed, except for the reality that so many families have been uprooted from this city due to years of extreme poverty and outright government neglect. It is now one of the ten poorest cities in America. It reminds me of a ghost town with so many abandoned properties left in ruins. Of the families that remain here, many are hanging on with bare minimum support. The city's poor have been exploited for as long as I can remember; that was a major contributing factor to the high crime rate in Newburgh. Several years ago there was a growing problem of gang activity in the community, but the FBI and State Police have since 2010 come in to eradicate much of the city's gang activity. Mass incarceration of Black and brown youth has always been a quick fix for urban problems, but if you ask most of the people in inner city communities they would tell you that the real criminals are still at large, still pocketing federal and state dollars that were earmarked for housing programs and other development projects for these slums.

Because so many Black and brown poor youth are incarcerated and so many slumlords have gotten away with renting uninhabitable apartments, or raising rents above the actual poverty level incomes of ghetto families, many people have been forced out of their homes. When this happens, often simultaneously, herds of gentrifiers storm the neighborhood scouting abandoned properties for quick fixer-uppers to put back on the market for a more desirable higher income population. This is the unfortunate reality. It becomes even sadder to know that Black people here have not learned any lessons from this urban crisis. Many of them are so demoralized that they have no idea where to begin helping themselves, even if they tried. The few past activists in Newburgh are exhausted or now deceased, so the message to vote and to be socially active is not heard enough.

I come back to this city not expecting any happy rendezvous or nostalgic experience. I know what it is and what to expect from this place. No one I knew is here – not anyone that I can relate to or who I could talk to about life outside of Newburgh. For those who remain here, I want to believe they have enough imagination left for my own story to somehow inspire them to escape this sad city. I'm no superman. I am far from that. But in-between the ghosts who roam in and out of these abandoned apartment buildings and those who do remain living in this city I want to share with them my story and to let them know that I too know what it feels like living inside a place that is difficult to call home. I want them to feel empowered enough to call this city a prison that suffocates their dreams and the dreams of the children who live here. I want them to realize that they deserve better. They deserve more than the broken concrete underneath their feet and the shattered windows all around them. But most people here are still very distrusting of people they don't know. So they avoid eye contact as they walk past me. My simple "Hello" or "Peace" is almost always ignored. They are on the move. Everyone here is. Meaningful dialogue has very little place where people are trying to make it to tomorrow. They have been let down so many times that they expect nothing from anyone and they feel undeserving of anything good. So they take what they can when they can. The last thing they are open to is some superman attempting to save them. Even if that superman was here to tell them that they must become their own heroes and save themselves.

CHAPTER 52

THE SEED

THE SEED Public Charter School of Washington, DC, is a unique place that my wildest imagination about school reform and academic instruction of urban youth could never imagine. At the State University of New Paltz I had earned a Masters Degree in Humanistic/Multicultural Education and knew all about the inequalities of urban classrooms. My own experience in the Newburgh, NY, public school system where teachers had blatantly marked off me and my peers as future social derelicts, if not dead by 21, was very useful background experience. My life was coming full circle. In my darker days I could never believe that I would become a teacher. My earlier life was definitely haunted by the messages of white and sometimes Black teachers in charge of my early education who counted me out and predicted that the ghetto would eventually consume me in the same way that it had consumed a generation of young Black men before me. Now I was employed as a non-traditional educator in a 24-hour learning environment. The 300-plus students the school housed in dormitories five nights a week were referred to as scholars. The majority of these young scholars, male and female, were from South East D.C. and almost all African-American. The school is a public boarding program that instructs students in the 6th through 12th grade, and because of the boarding program I would get to know these students in ways that some of their own parents would not as I tried to teach them reading, writing, study habits and life skills beyond the classroom.

In my first year at the SEED School I was able to launch a photography Spark Program with a handful of middle school students, and start a book club that was at first a serious challenge because most of the students in the class either could not read or were afraid to read in public. The other issue that I soon discovered was that because some of the students had difficulty reading, they made excuses that my selection of literature wasn't entertaining enough for them. Illiteracy and the facade of gangsterism usually went hand and hand with urban students who refused to be spotted as the kid who couldn't read in class. My solution for keeping the classroom focused was to offer snacks during reading, select the strongest readers among the group, and to find the most entertaining pieces of literature I could imagine. Nothing came easy with this group. It was always a matter of my giving something to them long enough to receive just a moment of their fiery yet fleeting attention. But in those priceless moments we were able to complete the reading of the book "Monster" by Sanyika Shakur, a case study of the life of young Robert Sandifer, and we made it halfway through the autobiography of Malcolm X. They were able to find meaning in the material by relating to worlds that were similar to their own. Sanyika Shakur had politicized their urban reality. The tragic demise of Robert Sandifer showed them how easy it was for adolescents to be swayed down negative paths in life. The autobiography of Malcolm X was quite a challenge for these seventh and eighth graders because the context of Malcolm's life on the surface seemed extremely different from what my students live daily in South East, DC. I was hoping that Malcolm's transformation from criminal to one of the most eloquent orators and greatest civil rights litigators ever would inspire them to realize that education was a weapon for personal change.

The highlight of my time working with middle schoolers was my daily Hip Hop session where we would listen to classic and modern rap songs and formulate discussions around the lyrics. Talk about eye opening revelations! We were able to discern the spirituality of some of the most crass rap songs and establish that rappers such as Future and Kodak Black were spitting Ghetto Gospels that were just as relevant as any preacher's sermon. These rap sessions also gave the participating students an opportunity to freestyle their own versions of their everyday challenges growing up as teens in D.C. I have probably learned more from them than I have taught them, and I've learned more about myself than I had expected from these unorthodox interactions. Each generation of students reacts differently to the issues and crises of their day, and they learn how to create their own means of survival that is packed into their generation's very own lexicon and ideology. These children, despite the socio-economic conditions that they were born into, are no less intelligent than the generations of youth before them. I would argue that they are equally intelligent and just as resilient. And my students grew up under the eight-year term of President Barack Obama and his theme of the audacity of hope. Juxtapose what this generation believes is rightfully due to them, in terms of respect and liberty and fair treatment and employment opportunities under the law, with those terrifying incidents of police brutality in Ferguson of 2014 and in Baltimore of 2015 and you will see that today's generation of youth has proven to be as socially engaged as those who marched on Washington in 1963.

Teaching at the SEED School in Washington taught me that there are much better ways to educate inner city students across America than the way I was told by my white grade school teacher that I would not live to be 21. As educators we have to walk into each and every classroom space and assume that our students are full of enormous potential to become their greatest Self. We have to believe that students, especially the Black and brown ones, are just as hungry for inspiring dialogue and education as other students, and that Black and brown students are deserving of enriching academic instruction.

I had the opportunity to work with the high schoolers at SEED. Those were personally rewarding moments for me. I would take them on tours to visit college campuses and on trips throughout the District of Columbia. I also became one of the instructors in the Niarchos Greece Scholars Program where I instructed high school students on Ancient and modern Greek culture and history. The program allowed those students who successfully completed the coursework an opportunity to travel to Greece for two weeks. I would be one of the chaperones accompanying the students. I taught in the program for two years and traveled to Greece for two summers.

This was huge for the students but a major accomplishment for me as well. I was doing something meaningful with my life and I was positively impacting students I saw as younger versions of myself who were heading down the wrong path in life if intervention didn't happen. I was that new man, a transformed vessel of change and Black love. My very own narrative from prisoner to educator, transformed by the power of self-education, self-knowledge, and self-love, is my driving force. It is my purpose. It is my calling. I survived the Belly of the Beast to be here today to tell a story to Black and brown youth that our presence here on this planet is possible, is permanent, and does not have to be shadowed by the fear of extinction. I am here to tell these young students, wherever I find them, that an authentic Black love is the only true weapon against the hegemony of white racism.

Black love is not anti-white. It is positive rejection of any force that denies Black development, Black achievement, Black excellence. It secures permanency. It reminds us that we are not disposable. It enlightens the world and instructs others that we too are good enough to be embraced and respected and not feared. No doubt about it, we are the black salt of the earth. I will continue to use my narrative to fight for inclusive communities and to educate the white eyes around me that they are responsible for developing language and political action that humanizes the urban experience. Without the humanity of whites working to improve the Black American urban experience, the ghetto is empty of the possibility of true freedom and reform. Without white support we remain caged birds fantasying about freedom from behind social and economic bars. We cry of freedom but will never truly experience freedom until white eyes are no longer fearful of becoming stung by black salt.

(above) Margaret Johns. (below) Painting by Nasihah Jones of dead bodies on the ground with bullet shells attached to some bodies.

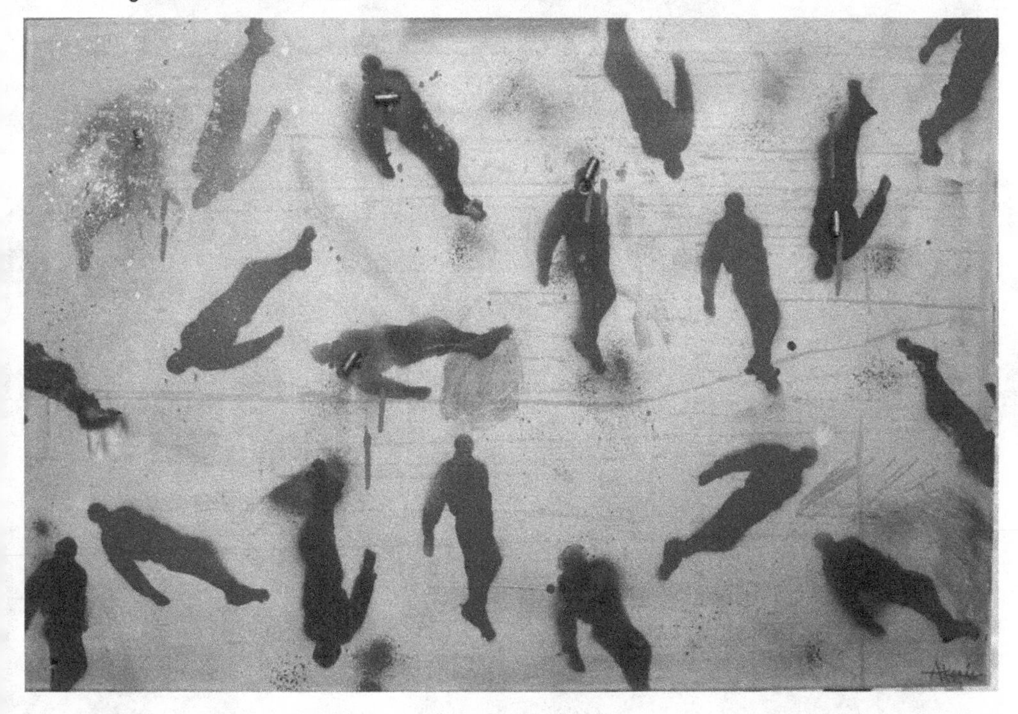

(left) Candid photo of homeless man walking (2011). (above) "After Libations" Makeshift memorial marking the death of an unknown individual (2015). (below) "Death Celebration." Makeshift memorial marking the death of an individual (2015).

In American ghettos, when someone is killed it is a tradition to hang their shoes on electric wires near the shooting. 2009.